The *Electronic Trading of Options*

Maximizing Online Profits

HOWARD ABELL

DEARBORN™
A **Kaplan Professional** Company

Associate Publisher: Cynthia Zigmund
Managing Editor: Jack Kiburz
Project Editor: Trey Thoelcke
Interior Design: Lucy Jenkins
Cover Design: Scott Rattray, Rattray Design
Typesetting: the dotted i

© 2000 by Innergame Partners

Published by Dearborn, a Kaplan Professional Company

Printed in the United States of America

00 01 02   10 9 8 7 6 5 4 3 2 1

Library of Congress Cataloging-in-Publication Data

Abell, Howard.
    The electronic trading of options / Howard Abell.
      p.   cm.
    Includes bibliographical references and index.
    ISBN 0-7931-3521-4
    1. Options (Finance)   2. Electronic trading of securities.   I. Title.
  HG6024.A3 A243   2000
  332.63'228—dc21   99-049648

DEDICATION

This book is dedicated to all traders who have the courage and the knowledge to pursue their vision of "free enterprise."

OTHER BOOKS BY HOWARD ABELL

The Market Savvy Investor

Digital Day Trading

Risk Reward

Day Trader's Advantage

Spread Trading

CONTENTS

FOREWORD

In the beginning, there was outcry; the act of one man yelling at many and many yelling at one in order to communicate in a marketplace. This was the primal and sole method to communicate one's desire to buy and sell the product at issue. Open outcry flourished in an organized fashion for over 100 years.

Then came silicon—a derivative of the natural resource sand—which led to the development of the revolutionary computer chip that we have seen transform so many facets of our lives. For one, it has created significant inroads to this ancient method of open outcry or pit trading.

Over the past decade that International Trading Institute has serviced the electronic markets, we've had the opportunity to both participate in, and witness the proliferation of this phenomenon. We have worked with the representatives of over 30 countries since 1989, concentrating our efforts on educating market participants about derivative products to assist their marketplaces to flourish into sophisticated trading arenas.

Now, ten years later, we have seen a role reversal. We are now learning from seasoned electronic trading veterans, as we begin to incorporate the use of electronic execution systems and the implementation of electronic exchanges here in the United States.

In August 1987, we saw the opening of the first electronic futures and options exchange, SOFFEX (Swiss Options and Financial Futures Exchange). Soon after, the DTB (Deutsche Terminbörse) followed suit, introducing a different flavor of the same electronic trading platform. Electronic markets began emerging all over the world, continuing to advance and being perfected technologically with each step. Recently, various electronic exchanges have taken it even further by forming alliances that provide for cross border, electronic trading.

While this quiet revolution took place outside the U.S. borders, America experienced a propagation of electronic trading of only equities. A contingent does exist that doubts the United States will ever completely do away with open outcry for options. Others believe our markets will accommodate side-by-side trading for some time (the ability to trade products in the pit and electronically simultaneously).

Similar doubts were prevalent in the early '90s when the DTB first launched the BUND contract (German Government Bond) on it's electronic platform, competing for market share directly with the Liffe (London Financial Futures Exchange) floor traders. This was viewed as the barometer for measuring the viability of electronic vs. floor trading as it was the first time automated trading competed directly with open outcry.

As we go to press, the DTB's market share (now Eurex) for the BUND (now EuroBund) is 100 percent and the Liffe no longer trades it.

Because of our first-hand experiences globally, we are often asked, how long until the United States transitions to a fully electronic marketplace?

Although we have experienced the evolution of an electronic marketplace for equities in the United States over the past couple of years, it is our opinion that it would require a combination of factors be in place for this revolution to take place for options trading. Technology would have to progress to a level that could handle the exponentially large quote dissemination of the U.S. derivatives markets, and a methodology would have to be devised that could cope with the culturally ingrained acceptance and tradition of open outcry. As we approach a new millennium, however, it does appear that the two forces, massive derivatives trading in open cry markets and sophisticated technology, are on a collision course.

The Electronic Trading of Options is intended to be a resource for those individuals in need of an explanation as to what opportunities and technology are presently available to trade options as either a professional market participant or as an individual investor. In addition, included is an introduction to options trading, for those who are new to options.

As a contributor to this book, we offer no exact prognostication as to when the vast world of options trading may be fully electronic. However, as we advance technologically it seems that the momentum is here. In fact, as we have seen most recently with Eurex, cross-exchange trading capabilities via the advent of international electronic exchange alliances introduces yet another realm of derivatives trading: one global electronic exchange.

Karen E. Johnson
President
International Trading Institute

PREFACE

Around the world, exchanges are abandoning traditional trading floors for cheaper, faster, and directly accessible computer systems that match buyers and sellers electronically. It's already happened in Australia, England, and France, and it's just a matter of time before online trading becomes the industry standard in options as it has with equities.

The Electronic Trading of Options: Maximizing Online Profits identifies and explains to traders and investors some of the revolutionary changes that are now occurring in the financial arena and reveals everything that is required for traders and investors to profitably trade options electronically. In addition, I have made every effort to point out the best possible sources of education and training for the serious student of options (both novice and seasoned investor), as well as to identify cutting edge software that will enable him or her to compete on a level playing field with professional market makers.

Specifically, *The Electronic Trading of Options* reveals:

1. The electronic trading platforms already in existence and the new ones to be launched beginning in the year 2000.

   • Eurex (European Electronic Exchange)

   • Globex (Chicago Mercantile Exchange)

   • CX (Cantor Exchange)

   • Liffe Connect

   • ISE (International Securities Exchange)

   • Chicago Board Options Exchange (CBOE)

2. The state-of-the-art trading systems available to options traders now and those that will be available in the near future: the look of their screens and windows and their operating instructions.

3. How to become a successful electronic options trader: identifying and describing specific technical, mechanical, and tactical skills.

4. The new options trading necessity: sophisticated options trading training and familiarizing oneself with front-end risk management and order execution systems.

5. The basic options strategies from a traditional and electronic perspective.

6. How seasoned trading pros like Tony Saliba, Chris Hausman, and Joe Corona view the new electronic trading arena and what their recommendations for trading options profitably are.

7. How traders and investors can use technical analysis to identify option trading opportunities.

8. How to put it all together: the psychological and investment tools that are required to trade options successfully.

Everywhere possible I have tried to keep one overriding concern at the forefront: to write a practical options trading manual for hedgers and speculators that provides solid, basic theory but never loses sight of investors' primary concern—bottom-line performance.

The Electronic Trading of Options is the logical sequel to *Digital Day Trading* and provides an invaluable resource for option traders and sophisticated investors about market philosophy and trading strategy, given the new technological realities of the electronic financial arena. It also offers specific technical and tactical methods, bolstered by considerations of money and risk management, which can significantly strengthen a trader's overall market performance.

Success in trading and investing.

ACKNOWLEDGMENTS

I wish to thank the many people who have made significant contributions to the writing of *The Electronic Trading of Options*. The success of this book is a testament to their generosity of time and mind, as well as their good humor and understanding when it came to rewrites and deadlines. Outstanding talents and fertile minds have made writing this book most enjoyable. They are: Karen Johnson, President of International Trading Institute; Tony Saliba, Chris Hausman, Joe Corona, and Elizabeth Regan of Eurex; Debra Walton of Cantor Fitzgerald; and Morgan McKenney of Liffe Connect. In particular, I wish to thank my business partner, Bob Koppel, for his many fine ideas and suggestions, all which were taken.

I wish also to thank Roslyn Kolin Abell, wife and friend, for her insights and strong support. Finally I would like to acknowledge Cynthia Zigmund and the entire staff at Dearborn Trade: their ongoing commitment to and enthusiasm for this project are gladly noted.

PART ONE

THE NEW REALITY OF OPTIONS TRADING

1

THE CHANGING
FINANCIAL
LANDSCAPE

In the past few years the financial markets have undergone tremendous changes. A host of new products and financial instruments have been introduced against a backdrop of a new technology that seems to make revolutionary advances daily.

The digital age of investment has arrived. Hal Hansen, former Chairman of the Futures Industry Association recently said, "Eventually, electronic networks will replace a significant part, if not all, of the trading activity in Chicago." Individual traders and investors, strengthened by knowledge of computers and an ability to quickly click information and services into their perceptual field of vision, are comfortable with the idea of bypassing brokers to enter the rarefied arena of the major Wall Street players.

Dave Petit, a *Wall Street Journal* editor, remarked, "The rush to go online promises to dramatically change the nature of individual investing both for the investors themselves and the businesses that cater to them." For individuals, online investing has meant a chance to take full responsibility for their finances:

You execute your own trades without a broker to hold your hand. The Internet also has provided a radically cheaper way to invest.

Until the 1970s, the securities industry was conducted in its own time-honored fashion. The brokerage houses controlled the flow of orders, made largely to the New York Stock Exchange (NYSE), but to a lesser degree to the American Stock Exchange (AMEX) and the over-the-counter market (OTC). Not only was the order flow controlled, but the commissions charged to the general public were fixed. Price reporting was available at your broker's office or in newspapers, and only professional securities traders or high net worth individuals had real-time access to price and volume information.

In 1971 the National Association of Securities Dealers created Nasdaq, an electronic market where members could display their bids and offers to other members. On May 1, 1975, fixed commissions were terminated by Securities and Exchange Commission (SEC) decree; a new era of competitive pricing and discount brokerage was born. The termination of fixed commissions, which was the culmination of a five-year phase-out (and said at the time to be the death knell of the securities industry), actually turned out to be the main ingredient in the subsequent explosion of trading volume. An industry that had predicted brokerage house failures and the end of the industry saw a new breed of brokerage house, called "discount brokers," provide an increased order flow at greatly reduced prices. Not only were discount brokers profitable, but they generated the explosion in trading volume by making the cost of buying and selling an insignificant factor.

Over the years and with some SEC rules changes, the Nasdaq system has evolved from a members only, inside market, to a quotation platform open to all. In 1985 the Small Order Execution System (SOES) was introduced to allow customers to buy on an offer and sell on a bid for up to a thousand

shares at a time. After the 1987 crash, when market makers re-
fused to answer phones or backed away from their quotes,
Nasdaq instituted an automatic electronic execution system
through SOES. Soon after, the SelectNet system was created,
which allowed customers to see and trade with market maker
bids and offers as well as other customers' bids and offers.

The final ingredient in the explosion in the securities industry is online access to the markets that is readily available to
all, at a cheap cost, with state-of-the-art quickness and preci-
sion. Today's technology offers the buying and selling of stock
via the Internet, bypassing a broker and accessing inexpensive
online systems. Such systems not only supply quotes and
news, but also allow the direct entry of orders through participation in the SelectNet system and the various electronic communication networks (ECNs) that present your bids and offers
on an equal footing with other market professionals.

Online trading can mean Internet, the Web, or any available means of transmitting orders and information, such as
private network, satellite, TV, or even pager technology. In the
time between the conception of this book and the writing of
this chapter, trading technology continued to make extraordi-
nary advances. Changes ranged from simple Internet order
entry access to securities markets, to electronic networks
available at brokerage sites, to total market access on the
trader's personal computer (PC). Technologies changed daily.
As an example, online trading access began as a method to get
delayed quotes on your PC, type in an order to buy or sell a security, and send that order to your broker, who would then forward it to be executed. Then traders had the ability to obtain
live quotes inexpensively, enter orders and receive fills directly from the markets that the security trades on, and have at
their fingertips many management tools to organize their port-
folios and enhance money management. Following that, new
styled brokers emerged, supplying computer stations with the

most advanced software and instant access to all markets via Nasdaq level 2 and the various electronic networks, offering information and account management tools in many cities across the nation.

Now, the technology that was available only at the brokers' offices is available online on your PC for a reasonable fee on a fee-for-service basis. Real-time market quotes, charts, news, ticker alerts, one button order entry, and almost instantaneous order execution are now a click away, with excellent reliability.

THE WORLD OF ELECTRONIC TRADING

SuperDot

SuperDot is the electronic platform for listed markets. Almost 40 percent of the shares traded on the NYSE in any day is executed on SuperDot. This system can handle up to 99,999 share orders. This system links member firms to the specialists on the floor of the exchange.

Although SuperDot usually is not available to individuals, there are several other systems offering similar access to the markets.

Electronic Communications Networks (ECNs)

Instinet, Island, Bloomberg, and Teranova are ECNs available to everyone. Traders, market makers, and institutions can have their bids or offers displayed and thereby make a market on Nasdaq stocks. Through ECN order entry terminals and/or your own PC, you can now participate in the entire Nasdaq market on an equal basis with market professionals.

At the present time, the Nasdaq market offers the best opportunity for the day or swing trader to compete. Because listed securities traded on the NYSE, AMEX, and other exchanges in the United States and around the world, are still traded within a specialist system, and traders do not have direct access to buyers and sellers and so lose much of their edge in short-term trades. This does not mean there is no opportunity in the listed markets. There are many good trades and many interesting stocks to include in one's portfolio, however, the trader must adapt methods to the different system.

It is more important to develop a consistent, disciplined approach to trading based on the information available in the market in terms of price and other statistics than worry about whether it's a specialist, market maker, hedge fund, or Joe Trader that is on the other side of your trade.

HOW TO BEGIN

Hardware

Almost any computer purchased in the past two years should have the capability to put you online. The minimum requirements for online trading are Pentium chip or equivalent 133 MHz, 32 MB RAM, 28 bps or higher modem, and 1 gigabyte or more hard drive memory.

Some software that includes live NYSE, AMEX, and Nasdaq quotes; Nasdaq level 2 display; live technical charts; custom studies; position manager; point and click execution panel; and custom "hot" keys may have higher minimum online requirements.

A computer with a faster chip and/or modem than the on-line minimum, and/or more RAM, will increase your efficiency and make your life easier. If your intention is to day trade actively, then the higher level of hardware is well worth the additional expense.

Software

There are different categories of software. They are:

- *Internet access.* This software is provided by an Internet service provider (ISP) and provides the ability to connect your PC to the Internet through the ISP's server.

- *Internet browser.* The two most common browser companies are Microsoft and Netscape. Microsoft's Internet Explorer is included in your Microsoft PC operating system and Netscape can be downloaded directly from the Internet.

- *Order entry software.* This software is provided by the brokerage company that holds your account. It sends orders and receives fills; it may keep track of your trades; show you your portfolio; provide quotes, news, charts, market maker screens, and tickers; and supply research reports.

- *Analysis software.* There are many choices for software that contain various technical studies or will allow you to create your own. Some of this software also will allow you to test what you create or test a combination of studies that are included in the software. An example is Options Pro by Omega Research.

Product manufacturers and vendors who are actively soliciting your business make finding and getting acquainted with your requirements easier. Pick up any business newspaper or magazine or turn on a local or national financial news station on radio or TV and you will have much to choose from.

OPTIONS TRADING

With the expansion and growth of the options market, exciting changes also are occurring for investors. In 1973, options that are exchange listed, government regulated, and standardized became available. They were first traded on the Chicago Board Options Exchange (CBOE). Within a decade, the daily volume of trading in equities options had often exceeded the numbers of shares underlying the options that were traded on the NYSE. A similar pattern also exists in the futures industry where the markets have grown in large part because of the introduction of options on futures.

OPTIONS DEFINED

Options are known as derivative instruments; that is, the value of an option is based on the underlying stock, bond, index, or currency, etc. In reality, traders of derivative instruments are also traders in the underlying security, index, financial, or agricultural instrument because price moves in the derivatives often—but not always—closely reflect or parallel what is occurring in the primary market.

Although the general investor often sees options, like most derivatives, as highly speculative instruments, they are in fact an important risk management tool: allowing hedgers and producers to transfer risk and speculators to assume risk. The hedger's main concern is to establish a specific price level to "lock in" a price against a price base or sale in a particular market. Theoretically the speculator takes on the price risk that the hedger seeks to minimize. The important thing for the investor to keep in mind when trading options is that because they do involve risk, consistent profit making requires adherence to time-tested, market-proven rules of disciplined speculation and money management.

RULES OF DISCIPLINED SPECULATION AND MONEY MANAGEMENT

For options investors—hedgers and speculators—to have successful outcomes, they must adhere to these 12 rules:

1. *Define your loss.* Establish your maximum draw-down.

2. *Have a well-defined money management program.* Develop a system that provides for consistency, never risking more than 2 percent of your capital on any given trade.

3. *Don't trade with emotion.* The more emotional content that you can eliminate from your trading, the higher probability of a successful outcome.

4. *Focus on opportunities.* Learn which are the essentials of the market you are following and learn how to discriminate the signal from the noise. And know how

much noise-to-signal risk is tolerable, what Warren Buffet refers to as "quotational risk."

5. *Trade with a consistent methodology at your areas of opportunity.* The trader needs to be aggressive and consistent when a well-analyzed opportunity that is congruent to his or her methodology materializes.

6. *Trade in the correct state of mind.* There is an optimal performance state for trading and investing, which my partner Bob Koppel described in detail in *The Tao of Trading* (Dearborn, 1998). It includes the following:

- The trader is physically relaxed.

- The trader is psychologically calm.

- The trader approaches the market with optimism.

- The trader possesses an energized demeanor.

- The trader is actively engaged with the market.

- The trader has a sense of play, gaming, or "fun" about the market.

- The trader makes decisions and executes trades effortlessly.

- The trader trades without anxiety.

- The trader's reaction to the market is automatic— without hesitation or regret.

- The trader is alert and available to all market actions.

- The trader is highly confident.

- The trader feels in control of all actions taken in the market.

- The trader is highly concentrated and focused on market essentials.

- The trader moves in and out of the market without the intrusion of ego.

That is, the trader does not make decisions based on factors external to the market.

7. *Don't overtrade.* The trader needs to take only high probability "set-ups." These trades may be based on chart patterns, computer numbers, or historical price and volatility, as is the case with options.

8. *Don't average a loss.* This is invariably a losing strategy.

9. *Take small losses, large profits.* The trader must adhere to a methodology that allows this to occur. A 3-to-1 ratio of profit-to-loss is what most professional traders look for.

10. *Have no bias to either side of the market.* Trading with options allows you to develop bull and bear strategies. The trader must be poised to exploit market opportunities on either side of the market and not be a "one way trader."

11. *Preserve capital.* Trader must have a clear understanding of the difference between well-calculated and un-calculated risk taking. Successful speculation is the result of carefully planned, well-analyzed systems and consistent risk management.

12. *Think in probabilities.* The successful options trader has a well-defined boundary of operations that is based on probability so that the trader may act decisively at key

entry and exit points. Remember that successful trading is the direct result of a well-disciplined approach of calculated risk taking that is based on high probability trades. Again the purpose of operating with a high-probability, well-defined boundary is to allow the trader to do the following:

- Effectively manage emotions

- Overcome the pitfalls of crowd psychology

- Understand his or her conscious and unconscious motivations

- Calculate an appropriate percentage of the overall portfolio

- Maintain a systematic and consistent approach

- Resist trades that are outside a defined risk parameter

- Calculate additional viable risk opportunities

- Trade in a manner that is analytical and disciplined in every stage of the investment process.

As you read over each item above, ask yourself the following questions:

- How does this discussion of the successful principles of speculation relate to me?

- How do I personally experience risk?

- What emotion (physical and psychological) do I have when assuming risk in the market?

- What specific investment anxieties do I have and how can I overcome them?

- What am I thinking about when I take a loss in the market and how does that help or inhibit my market performance?

- What self-defeating attitudes do I possess that I can overcome to trade more effectively?

- How can I best use the information contained in *The Electronic Trading of Options* to enhance my trading method?

Now that we have an understanding of what is required of the options trader on a daily basis in terms of individual preparation, turn to Chapter 2 to learn about options essentials: What makes options unique as investment vehicles and how they can be used to enhance the bottom line and minimize risk to the options hedger and speculator.

2

OPTIONS
ESSENTIALS

Again, the two broad categories of investors who can benefit from investing in options are hedgers and speculators. The hedger transfers risk to the speculator who then assumes it. Let's first look at the hedger. Why would an individual or firm choose to hedge—to "lock in" price protection? It is the hedger's risk management; when investing in options it is insurance. Options provide the following benefit:

- An option provides protection against falling prices for the seller of the underlying instrument.

- An option provides protection against rising prices for those who plan to buy.

- An option protects an existing position in a security or future.

Specifically then, the benefits of options to the investor seeking price protection can be easily understood as follows:

- The investor can protect equity holdings from a decline in stock market price.

- The investor can increase income using current stock holdings.

- The investor can prepare to buy a stock at a lower price.

- The investor can position oneself for a significant market move, even if the direction the market will move is unknown.

- The investor can benefit from a rise in a stock or future price without incurring the cost of buying the underlying instrument.

Speculation in options is assuming the risk that is transferred by the individual or firm that has established a hedge. But what precisely are options?

OPTIONS DEFINED

An option, whether on equities (stock options) or futures (options on futures) is literally a contract that provides its holder with the right (but not the obligation) to buy or sell shares or contracts (futures) of the underlying security or product at a specified price on or before a given date. Once this date has passed, the option expires. An option contract, therefore, specifies three conditions:

1. The property to be delivered

2. The price of the property

3. A specified period during which the buyer has the right to exercise the option

Options are standardized instruments with terms, exercise price, and expiration time. This standardization allows buyers and writers (sellers) of options to close out their positions by offsetting sales and purchases by selling an option with the same terms as the one purchased, or buying one with the same terms as the one sold. An investor can thus liquidate a position at any time.

WHY TRADE OPTIONS?

Options are very versatile investment vehicles for individuals and institutions that understand the risks and limitations. Options strategies allow for more than just buying or selling. Options allow investors to configure their positions to individual market conditions and situations, using conservative or aggressive strategies as deemed appropriate.

Options can be used to take a position in the market in an effort to capitalize on an upward or downward market move. Unlike stocks, however, options can provide an investor the benefits of leverage over a position in an individual stock or basket of stocks reflecting the broad market. At the same time, options buyers also can take advantage of predetermined, limited risk. Conversely, options writers assume significant risk if they do not hedge their positions.

CALLS AND PUTS

A call is the right to buy the stock, while a put is the right to sell the stock. The person, who purchases an option, whether it is a put or a call, is the option "buyer." Conversely the person who originally sells the put or call is the option "seller."

To the buyer, an equity call option normally represents the right to buy 100 shares of underlying stock, whereas an equity put option normally represents the right to sell 100 shares of underlying stock. The seller of an option is obligated to perform according to the terms of the options contract—selling the stock at the contracted price (the strike price) for a call seller, or purchasing it for a put seller—if the option is exercised by the buyer.

All option contracts traded on U.S. securities exchanges are issued, guaranteed, and cleared by the Options Clearing Corporation (OCC). OCC is a registered clearing corporation with the Securities and Exchange Commission (SEC) and has received a AAA credit rating from Standard & Poor's Corporation. The AAA credit rating corresponds to OCC's ability to fulfill its obligations as counter party for options trades. (The OCC will be discussed in Chapter 3)

The Chicago Board Options Exchange (CBOE) is the world's largest options market and the nation's second largest securities exchange. Options also are traded on the American Stock Exchange (AMEX), the New York Stock Exchange (NYSE), the Pacific Stock Exchange (PSE), and the Philadelphia Stock Exchange (PHLX). Investors can contact these exchanges at the following addresses:

Chicago Board Options
   Exchange
400 South LaSalle Street
Chicago, IL 60605
800-OPTIONS
www.cboe.com

American Stock Exchange
Options Marketing Dept.
86 Trinity Place
New York, NY 10006
800-THE AMEX
www.amex.com

New York Stock Exchange
Options and Index Products
20 Broad Street
New York, NY 10005
800-692-6973
www.nyse.com

Philadelphia Stock Exchange
1900 Market Street
Philadelphia, PA 19103
800-THE PHLX
www.phlx.com

Pacific Stock Exchange
Options Marketing
220 Montgomery, #201
San Francisco, CA 94104
800-TALKPSE
www.pacificex.com

Options are not limited to common stock. They are written on bonds, currencies, commodities, and various indexes (e.g., S&P 100, etc.). The CBOE trades options on listed and over-the-counter (OTC) stocks, on Standard and Poor's (S&P) 100 and 500 market indexes, on U.S. Treasury bonds and notes on long-term and short-term interest rates, and on foreign currencies.

Options traded on exchanges such as the CBOE share both similarities and differences with common stock. Figure 2.1 illustrates points of comparison and contrasts.

BASIC TERMINOLOGY

The terms that follow represent the basic language of options trading. Understanding the significance of each of these terms is critical for undertaking even the most basic strategies.

FIGURE 2.1   A Comparison of Options with Common Stocks

Similarities	*Differences*
1. Options are listed securities.	1. There is no fixed number of options. The number of available options is solely contingent on the number of buyers and sellers.
2. Executed orders to buy and sell options are conducted in the same manner as orders to buy and sell stocks through a broker. Similar to common stock, orders on listed options are auctioned on the trading floor of a national exchange and can be sent via the Internet using an online broker.	2. There are no options certificates as evidence of ownership. Brokerage firms issue customer statements indicating ownership of options.
3. Price, volume, and other information about options is almost instantly available.	3. An option is a wasting asset. If it is not sold or exercised before it expires, it becomes worthless and the buyer loses the full purchase price paid for the "premium" or purchase price.
4. There is currently no direct electronic trading system for trading equity options for the general investor such as a Nasdaq level 2 system currently available to the general investor. However, this author believes with the introduction of ISE (International Securities Exchange) and proposed CBOE changes that this level of direct electronic trading will be available in 6–12 months.	4. Options, like common stocks, can be traded online but not currently on a fully electronic platform. Options on futures can be traded electronically on Globex, Eurex, and Liffe Connect.

As you read through these terms, keep in mind the two main advantages of options over other trading instruments:

1. *Leverage.* A relatively small investment controls a larger investment with corresponding increased profit or loss potential.

2. *Limited and defined risk.* Despite how much a particular stock or future falls in its underlying price, the investor's risk exposure is limited to the price of the premium. This is not true of the options writer who sells premium and thus does not have a limited or defined risk. With options, one additional point must be made: An investor may be correct in anticipating a future price change and still lose money because the price movement did not occur within the life span of the option.

The price of an option is called its "premium." The potential loss to the buyer of an option can be no greater than the initial premium paid for the contract, regardless of the performance of the underlying stock. This allows an investor to control the amount of risk assumed. On the other hand, the seller of the option, in return for the premium received from the buyer, assumes the risk of being assigned if the contract is exercised.

In accordance with the standardized terms of their contracts, all options expire on a certain date, called the "expiration date." For conventional listed options, this can be up to nine months from the date the options are first listed for trading. There are longer-term option contracts, called LEAPS, which can have expiration dates up to three years from the date of the listing. American-style options (the most commonly traded) and European-style options have different regulations relating to expiration and the exercising of an option. An American-style option is an option contract that may be exercised at any time between the date of purchase and the expiration date. A European-style option (used primarily with cash settled options) can only be exercised during a specified period of time just prior to expiration.

Call Options

The buyer of an American-style equity call option has purchased the right to buy 100 shares of the underlying stock at
the stated exercise price. Thus, the buyer of one XYZ June 110
call option has the right to purchase 100 shares of XYZ from
the seller at $110 up until June expiration. The buyer may do
so by filing an exercise notice through his or her broker or trading firm to the OCC prior to the expiration date of the option.
All calls covering XYZ are referred to as an "option class."
Each individual option with a distinctive trading month and
strike price is an "option series." The XYZ June 110 calls is an
individual series.

Put Options

The buyer of an American-style put option has purchased
the right to sell the number of shares of the underlying stock at
the contracted exercise price. Thus, the buyer of one ZYX June
50 put has the right to sell 100 shares of ZYX to the buyer at
$50 any time prior to the expiration date. In order to exercise
the option and sell the underlying stock at the agreed upon exercise price, the buyer must file a proper exercise notice with
the OCC through a broker before the date of expiration. All
puts covering ZYX stock are referred to as an "option class."
Each individual option with a distinctive trading month and
strike price is an "option series." The ZYX June 50 puts would
be an individual series.

How You Can Use Options

If you anticipate a certain directional movement in the price
of a stock, the right to buy or sell that stock at a predetermined
price, for a specific duration of time, can offer an attractive

investment opportunity. The decision as to what type of option to buy is dependent on whether your outlook for the respective security is positive (bullish) or negative (bearish). If your outlook is positive, buying a call option creates the opportunity to share in the upside potential of a stock without having to risk more than a fraction of its market value. Conversely, if you anticipate downward movement, buying a put option will enable you to protect against downside risk without limiting profit potential. Purchasing options offer you the ability to position yourself according to your market expectations in such a manner that you can both profit and protect with limited risk.

A detailed discussion of basic options strategies follows in Part 3.

- *Underlying.* The instrument (stock, future, or cash index) to be delivered when an option is exercised. The amount of underlying instrument for each option contract depends on the security traded. For example, in stock options each contract represents 100 shares of the underlying stock.

- *Exercise price.* The price at which the underlying instrument will be delivered in the event the option is exercised.

- *Exercise.* The process by which the buyer of an option notifies the seller of intention to take delivery of the underlying instrument in the case of a call, or make delivery, in the case of a put, at the specified exercise price.

- *Assignment.* The process by which the seller of an option is notified of the buyer's intention to exercise.

- *Expiration.* The date an option contract becomes null. A buyer of an option must indicate intent to exercise by this date.

- *American-style options.* Options that may be exercised before the expiration date.

- *European-style options.* Options that may be exercised during a specified expiration period.

- *In-the-money (ITM).* A call is in-the-money if its strike is lower than the market price of the underlying instrument. A put is in-the-money if its strike price is higher than the market price of the underlying instrument.

- *At-the-money (ATM).* An option whose exercise price is equal to the current market price of the underlying security.

- *Out-of-the-money (OTM).* An option that has no intrinsic value. A call is out-of-the-money if its strike price is greater than the current market price of the underlying instrument. A put is out-of-the-money if its strike price is lower than the current price of the underlying instrument.

- *Intrinsic value.* The amount by which an option is in-the-money. Out-of-the-money options have no intrinsic value.

- *Extrinsic value.* The price of an option less its intrinsic value. The entire premium of an out-of-the-money option consists of extrinsic value.

- *Long.* A position resulting from the purchase of a contract or instrument.

- *Short.* A position resulting from the selling of a contract or instrument. To sell a contract without, or prior to, exercising it.

- *Spread.* A long market position and an offsetting short market position usually, but not always, in contracts with the same underlying instrument.

- *Bull spread.* Any spread in which a rise in the price of the underlying security will theoretically increase the value of the spread.

- *Bear spread.* Any spread in which a decrease in the price of the underlying security will theoretically increase the value of the spread.

- *Neutral spread.* A position that has virtually no exposure to the conditions of a market. Also known as flat or square.

- *Delta.* The sensitivity (rate of change) of an option's theoretical value (assessed value) to changes in the price of the underlying instrument. Expressed as a percentage, it represents an equivalent amount price movement at a given time.

- *Gamma.* The sensitivity (rate of change) of an option's delta at a given time. It is most appropriate to use, expressed as the quantity of (underlying) instruments produced in a one strike move (equivalent to the basic value between two adjacent strike prices).

- *Rho.* The sensitivity of an option's theoretical value to a change in interest rates.

- *Vega.* The sensitivity of an option's theoretical value to a 1 percent change in volatility.

- *Theta.* The rate of decay of an option's theoretical value over one day.

- *Synthetics.* Two or more trading vehicles combined to emulate another, or a spread. Because the package involves different components, price is also different, but the risk is the same (there are exceptions, however).

- *Volatility.* The degree to which the price of an underlying instrument tends to change over time. This variable, which the market implies to the underlying instrument, may result from pricing an option through a model. Volatility is viewed from the positive side, which applies to the underlying instrument, and from the negative side, which applies to the option at any given moment in time.

Now that you have a basic familiarity with option terminology, in Chapter 3 we'll focus on how options are actually cleared between buyers and sellers, and hedgers and speculators. We'll also learn about the revolutionary changes occurring that will benefit the electronic option trader.

3

TRADING OPTIONS ELECTRONICALLY

The Options Clearing Corporation (OCC) is the largest clearing organization in the options industry and is regulated by the Securities and Exchange Commission (SEC). The OCC guarantees that the terms of an options contract (the specific stock, its price, and the specified period when the buyer may exercise) will be honored. In the option market, the OCC provides highly reliable clearance settlement and guarantee services. A wholly owned subsidiary, the Intermarket Clearing Corporation (ICC), provides a similar benefit to the futures industry.

It is the OCC that ultimately ensures performance to all buyers and writers of options, rather than any particular person or institution. In other words, once the OCC is satisfied that it is processing "matching" orders (the buyer and seller have traded the particular option and the premium has been paid), it becomes a direct link or clearing mechanism between the parties. It becomes the seller to the buyer and the buyer to seller. This is a process that benefits both the buyer and seller, with the OCC guaranteeing all options that it issues.

Founded in 1973 as the clearing corporation of the CBOE, the OCC currently clears trades for six organizations. They are the CBOE, AMEX, National Association of Securities Dealers (NASD), NYSE, PSE, and PHLX. The OCC is responsible for ensuring the financial integrity of the markets it clears, and protects the interests of its members. Therefore it has rigorous standards and safeguards in place, including membership standards, financial surveillance, market requirements, and a clearing fund. The OCC's mandate also includes:

- Monitoring the financial and operations conditions of each clearing member firm.

- Assessing on a daily basis general market conditions and the OCC's overall exposure with respect to member clearing firms.

- Evaluating the OCC's margins on a daily basis, and determining their adequacy to the prevailing market conditions.

For more information about the specific clearing and surveillance functions of the OCC, contact Options Clearing Corporation at www.cboe.com.

TECHNOLOGICAL CHANGES BENEFITING THE OPTIONS INVESTORS

The recent changes in the financial industry due to the introduction of online trading now also are available to the options trader. There are basically two current levels of electronic trading: (1) online and (2) electronic direct.

Online Options Trading

This level of service is available to the investor through a registered broker or dealer that primarily serves the function of an order taker. Let me explain. Historically there have been two levels of service available to the investor. The first was a full-service broker, providing a full range of customer services including trade recommendations, research material, and hands-on purchase and sale of customer orders including monitoring and reporting. Firms that still provide this level of service to the retail investor are: Merrill Lynch, Paine Webber, Prudential Securities, Dean Witter, and Shearson Lehman.

The second level of service is what used to be thought of as discount brokerage, designed primarily for investors who do their own research, make their own trading decisions, and as a result do not ordinarily require the assistance of a broker. The savings on this level of service can often be between 30 to 60 percent less than a full-service brokerage. Some routine services, however, still are provided. Examples of firms providing services at this level are Quick & Reilly and Muriel Siebert.

Today, with the advent of online trading there is a third level of brokerage service available to the investor that I call professional level. It is deeply discounted brokerage that is available to market savvy investors. It is designed for investors who have market expertise, make all their own trading decisions, and don't require broker assistance or advice. This level of service is available via the Internet for options trading on both securities and futures. Examples of firms that provide this level of service for options on securities are Brown & Co., E-Schwab, Wall Street Access, and Waterhouse Securities. For futures, there is First Options of Chicago, Rand Financial, and Lind-Waldock.

Opening an Account

A prospective investor must provide his or her name, address, occupation, Social Security number, citizenship, proof of age, and a bank or other financial reference. In addition, information on income, net worth, and investment experience also is required. The investor must acknowledge receipt of a disclosure document, that is, the current OCC prospectus, and sign an "Options Agreement," which verifies all submitted information on the account forms. Since 1975, commissions have been negotiable. Commissions usually are based on size of the account, as well as on volume and activity of business.

THE BASIC TYPE OF OPTIONS ORDERS

All options orders are considered day orders, meaning they are executable for that day only unless otherwise specified. An investor also can place "open" or "good until cancelled" (GTC) orders. The GTC order remains in effect until executed or cancelled. Options trading involves considerably more activity than trading in common stocks. Most listed options expire within nine months and many even more quickly. In addition, activity usually is based on adjusting positions as a result of changing volatility.

Market Order

A market order secures for the investor the best available price that is offered if you are a buyer and the best possible bid if you are a seller. For example, the price for an out-of-the-money call for stock XYZ is 7 bid at $7\frac{1}{4}$, and if you are a seller of the option you will be selling at 7. Market orders are used both for initiating and exiting positions. For investors who want to sell with the market makers or who don't want to "go to the market," there is the *limit order.*

Limit Order

The limit order stipulates that an option can only be executed at a specific price. For example, the investor places the order as follows: For an out-of-the-money call for XYZ stock, pay 7.

Stop Order

The stop order protects the investor against him- or herself. It is a kind of fail safe for the trader against the natural tendency to "wait and see." If the market goes beyond your risk limit, the stop order is executed and becomes a market order. For example, if you had bought the out-of-the-money call for XYZ at 7, to protect at least part of your investment you enter a sell stop at 4. The sell stop is converted into a market order as soon as the market ticks 4. The point here is that a stop order to sell becomes a market order when an option sells at or below the stop price (in this case 4, which is the premium). A stop order to buy becomes a market order when an option sells at or above the stop price.

Spread Orders

A spread order involves the purchase and sale of options on the same underlying stock, but with a different expiration date and/or a different exercise price. For example, you buy a June 50 call on XYZ stock and sell the June 60 call at the same time.

Straddle Orders

A straddle is the simultaneous purchase of a put and call on the same stock with the identical expiration price and expiration month. For example, you buy a June 50 call on XYZ stock and buy a June 50 put at the same time.

Ratio Spread Order

A ratio spread is the simultaneous purchase and sale of different quantities of calls or puts in the same underlying stock. For example, you buy a 1 June 50 call in XYZ stock and sell a 2 June 60 calls at the same time.

Strangles

A strangle is the simultaneous purchase of a call and a put with different strike prices. For example, you buy a June 50 put and buy a June 60 call.

Butterfly

A butterfly spread is the simultaneous purchase of a call, the sale of 2 calls at a higher price, and the purchase of a call at a still higher price. For example, you buy a June 50 call, sell 2 June 60 calls, and buy a June 70 call.

STRATEGY SELECTION

The choice of the appropriate option order is dictated by considerations of price, timing, volatility, and direction. In addition, the trader must factor in risk/reward characteristics of a particular trade, expected returns, and percent of equity invested in relationship to the total portfolio.

What follows here is a broad list of options trading strategies based on various market scenarios. This shows the types of orders and strategies that would be adopted in a given market condition. For example, if stable prices are anticipated in the near term, you could sell straddles or sell strangles.

Stable Prices	*Volatile Prices*
Sell Straddles	Buy Straddle
Sell Strangles	Buy Butterfly
Ratio Write	Buy Call
Short Butterfly	Buy Put
Ratio Spreads	Time Decay
	Tactics

Time Helps	*Time Hurts*	*Time Mixed*
Short Call	Long Call	Bull Spread
Short Put	Long Put	Bear Spread
Short Straddle	Long Straddle	Long Butterfly
Covered Call Write		Short Butterfly
Covered Put Write		

Profit/Loss Characteristics of Options Strategies

Strategy	*Profit Potential*	*Loss Potential*
Buy Call	Unlimited	Limited
Buy Put	Unlimited	Limited
Short Call	Limited	Unlimited
Short Put	Limited	Unlimited
Covered Call Write	Limited	Unlimited
Covered Put Write	Limited	Unlimited
Bull Spread	Limited	Unlimited

Bear Spread	Limited	Unlimited
Long Butterfly	Limited	Unlimited
Short Butterfly	Limited	Unlimited
Calendar Spread	Unlimited	Unlimited

ELECTRONIC DIRECT TRADING

The second level of electronic trading is electronic direct, currently only available to market makers and market professionals (an exchange member or an individual or institution that trades for or through an approved member of the clearing corporation). Electronic direct trading for options is comparable to what is currently available to equities traders on Nasdaq level 2. This professional level of trading will soon be generally available to sophisticated options traders for three reasons:

1. The relaxation of regulatory considerations

2. The introduction of electronic trading platforms such as Eurex and Liffe Connect, Globex, and CX

3. The inception of ISE, the International Securities Exchange, a fully automated electronic exchange and major new changes at the CBOE

Eurex

Eurex (EURopean EXchange) is the combined platform of Eurex Deutschland, the former DTB (Deutsche Terminborse), and Eurex Surich, the former Soffex (Swiss Options and Futures Exchange). Eurex operates a fully automated electronic options and financial futures trading and clearing system. In contrast to traditional open outcry exchanges, trading at Eurex is not conducted at a central location but via an electronic network. The market participants' computers and terminals are linked via access points—located in several cities in Germany as well as in Amsterdam, Chicago, Helsinki, London, Paris, and Zurich—to the Eurex host computer in Frankfurt. Exchange participants trade options and futures directly from their offices.

Eurex allows firms doing business in Euro (EUR), Swiss Franc (CHF), and Deutschmark (DM) instruments to benefit from the cost and time advantages associated with an exchange membership, regardless of their location. Eurex facilitates the efficient use of resources as all operations are fully automated and integrated. Trades are processed automatically and there are no out-trades. The system supports real-time risk management. Existing resources and trading experience can be leveraged by trading in additional markets in combination with established operations.

Currently Eurex lists options on 30 German and 17 Swiss blue chip stocks; futures and options on German, Swiss, and pan-European Index products; and interest rate products that cover the German yield curve from 1 month to 30 years and the Swiss yield curve from 3 to 13 years. Eurex Deutschland participants linking directly from the United States can trade only Commodity Futures Trading Commission (CFTC)-approved contracts, namely the DAX future and several of Eurex's fixed income Euro and DM denominated products (futures and options on futures for short-term, medium-term, and long-term German government bonds and 3-month Euromark futures).

Eurex became the largest futures and options exchange in 1999, with an average daily volume of 1,326,270 during the first quarter of 1999.

Participation in trading at Eurex via a terminal is possible in three different ways: as a (1) non-clearing member (NCM),

(2) a general clearing member (GCM), or (3) a direct clearing member (DCM) of Eurex. The difference between these memberships is their role in the clearing process.

Members from outside Germany or Switzerland only are admitted as NCMs. NCMs may execute trades for their own account or for their customers' accounts. They cannot clear and therefore require a clearing agreement with one of the 35 Eurex GCMs who may clear NCM business. Both GCMs and DCMs are allowed to clear their own trades and those of their customers, as well as business for their affiliates.

Eurex membership is granted by the exchange on admission and is nontransferable. There is no market for buying and selling Eurex memberships. To join Eurex, the company and each individual trader must apply for admission as an exchange participant (GCM, DCM, or NCM) or as a Eurex trader, respectively.

Admission as an Exchange Participant

Direct participation in trading on Eurex is possible if an institution has been admitted as a GCM, DCM, or NCM. The admission will be granted upon application, provided that the applicant fulfills the following main requirements for admission:

- *Registration of the company.* Eurex does not allow individual personal memberships. Companies must be officially registered in the state in which the member firm is located; for example, as a corporation, partnership, etc. Carrying out futures and options business would be stated as one of the company objectives in the articles of incorporation, the partnership agreement, etc.

- *Professional experience.* Persons acting on behalf of a Eurex member firm must provide their personal qualifications to conduct futures and options business, as well as their personal reliability. In addition, all traders need to pass the Eurex trader exam and give evidence of their familiarity with the Eurex trading system.

- *Technical conditions.* All Eurex members must comply with the exchange's technical requirements. The exchange member's EDP installation must allow the processing of trading and settlement through the exchange's EDP system.

- *Clearing.* Every Eurex member must guarantee the orderly processing of all transactions carried out on Eurex, in particular with respect to the clearing process. In accordance with Eurex rules and regulations, members from outside Germany or Switzerland are currently admitted as NCMs only. All trades executed directly via a Eurex terminal located in the offices of an NCM must be cleared through a Eurex GCM. Each NCM must therefore enter into a clearing agreement with a Eurex GCM located in either Germany or Switzerland. In addition, all NCMs must prove that they meet the Eurex minimum capital requirement of at least (EUR 51,000).

- *U.S. regulation.* U.S.–based Eurex Deutschland members only may conduct customer business on the exchange if they are registered as a futures commission merchant (FCM). FCM registration is not required if the firm engages in proprietary trading only. It should, however, be noted that relevant U.S. regulations apply to U.S.–based Eurex members.

- *Market making.* Eurex encourages market making by allowing every exchange participant to apply for admission as a market maker. The trader must provide evidence of his or her trading qualifications. When a market maker fulfills certain obligations, which vary from product to product, concessions on fees are granted by the exchange.

- *Admission as a Eurex trader.* Eurex members can have an unlimited number of traders at no additional cost. However, each individual Eurex trader must pass the Eurex trader examination and give evidence of his or her familiarity with the Eurex trading system. Examinations and preparatory courses for the examination, as well as systems trading courses, are offered on a regular basis in Frankfurt, London, Chicago, and New York City based on demand, examinations may be offered in other U.S. cities.

Study material for the trader examination is available from the exchange. Additional information may be secured by contacting Eurex at www.eurexchange.com.

Liffe Connect

Liffe Connect is a state-of-the-art electronic trading system that supports all Liffe exchange products. It has been designed to accommodate significant order flow and transaction volume in a highly reliable and time efficient manner. The combination of open system design and high performance capacity makes Liffe Connect a uniquely powerful and flexible electronic trading platform. In contrast to many existing electronic trading systems that require the purchase of specific computer hardware, Liffe Connect has an open architecture that allows traders to access the system through most standard desktop personal computers. This architecture also enables true customization of front-end trading software.

Rollout Schedule

The first release of Liffe Connect was delivered on schedule in November of 1998. The initial release featured the automated trading of individual equity options. Average daily volume during the first two months of this year was 17,524 contracts, 28 percent higher than floor volume during January and February 1998. On January 20, a record 35,486 equity options were traded on Liffe Connect. The exchange is actively working to build upon this success and a second release of Liffe Connect (release 2.0) automated bond and stock index futures during the second quarter of 1999. All bond and stock index futures, once placed onto Liffe Connect, will cease trading on the floor.

Version 2.1 of Liffe Connect, released in the third quarter of 1999, is specially designed to support trading of Liffe's money market futures contracts. Unlike the migration of its bond and stock index futures, the exchange intends to offer electronic trading of money market futures in parallel with the floor for as long as the market continues to express a preference for a choice of trading platforms. Global traders will therefore have the choice of transacting Euro futures on an electronic system with added functionality to support complex money market transactions or on the Liffe floor.

International Distribution

Liffe intends to distribute the system to international financial centers and will provide electronic subscribers with free access so long as they satisfy minimum volume levels. In order to facilitate direct access to Liffe Connect by international traders, Liffe will install network hubs in global financial centers, in accordance with the demands of Liffe members.

Network construction has begun with the installation of hubs in Chicago, New York, Frankfurt, and Paris.

The promulgation of final rules by the CFTC governing the distribution of trading terminals in the United States by foreign futures exchanges and approval on Liffe's specific application is currently pending. The exchange has maintained open lines of communication with the CFTC throughout this process and continues to work with the CFTC toward the release of final rules.

Access to Liffe Connect will be subscription based and not dependent on trading permits. The exchange has adopted the position that in an electronic trading environment it should not limit the number of individuals who have access to Liffe Connect once an institution becomes a member. One of many innovative design attributes of Liffe Connect is a powerful and state-of-the-art API (application programming interface) that allows choice in front-end trading applications. For this reason, Liffe is not providing international members with a stand-alone proprietary trading terminal, but rather access to a trading host through connections to a global network infrastructure. By severing the link between shareholding and market access, the exchange is allowing members to determine the number of staff that should have direct access to Liffe Connect and whether their customers should have indirect access through proprietary or third-party order routing systems. In this manner, all global traders will benefit from the flexibility implicit in the truly open architecture of Liffe Connect.

For more information about Liffe Connect and the specific products traded, contact Liffe at www.liffe.com. Products currently trading include:

5 and 10 year Dutch Gilts	FTSE 100, 250
FTSE Eurotop100	BTP
Bund	JGB
Euroyen	EFB 5 and 10 years
FTSE Eurobloc 100 Index	FTSE Eurotop 300 Index
FTSE Eurotop 300 EX UK Index	MSCI Pan Euro Index
3 Month Euribor	3 Month Euro Libor
Euroswiss	

Cantor Exchange (CX)

The CX is the first full-time electronic exchange for the trading of U.S. Treasury futures contracts. CX provides fast and direct links between traders and the exchange. Trades may be executed via direct keyboard access or by calling a CX terminal operator.

CX is owned by the New York Board of Trade (NYBOT) and its members. NYBOT was formed through the merger of the New York Cotton Exchange and the Coffee, Sugar & Cocoa Exchange, Inc., and brings more than 125 years of experience in building markets for futures.

Cantor Fitzgerald operates the trading platform for CX, utilizing the trading and distribution systems that have been perfected in Cantor Fitzgerald's highly liquid U.S. Treasury cash market. Cantor Fitzgerald pioneered the screen-based trading of U.S. government securities in 1972 and has since been at the forefront of electronic marketplace technology.

All trades executed on CX are cleared through the New York Clearing Corporation (NYCC), formerly the Commodity Clearing Corporation (CCC), the designated clearing organization of NYBOT. The NYCC represents more than 80 years of experience in clearing commodity futures and options contracts.

CX is regulated by the Commodity Futures Trading Commission.

On April 6, 1999, the CX began offering approved traders the choice of accessing the exchange via a terminal operator or via keyboard. Those eligible to execute trades electronically include NYCC members and their affiliates, full members of NYBOT, and market makers.

Traders who are approved by CX for futures trading and by Cantor Fitzgerald for cash trading may execute both futures and cash electronically on the same platform.

Futures Clearing Merchants (FCMs) may provide their customers and their employees with a choice of electronic or voice order routing, and an enhanced level of futures and cash execution, while preserving the anonymity of their customer relationships. FCM customer access can be facilitated by incorporating CX access into proprietary FCM front-end software.

By offering the choice of electronic or voice access to the exchange, CX aims to provide customers with a high level of service while building on the strengths of its proprietary electronic trading system, the new interactive Cantor Speed. Approved traders may choose to access CX via a dedicated Cantor Speed terminal, by integrating Cantor Speed into their own desktops using the Cantor Speed Application Programming Interface (API), or via a number of third-party providers.

Advantages of the Cantor Exchange include:

- *Anonymity.* CX never reveals the source of an order—minimizing market impact, leveling the playing field, and encouraging best price execution.

- *Lower trading and execution costs.* The electronic nature of CX eliminates the need for intermediaries in the trade execution process, enabling FCMs and clearing members who trade on CX to pass along potentially significant savings to their customers. The cost of trading on CX is significantly lower than in other markets.

- *Broad-based distribution of data and improved price transparency.* CX market data is available on Cantor Speed Systems via major market data vendors and (with a brief delay) on the Cantor Exchange Web site—reaching a broad audience.

- *Complete audit trails and records.* CX provides extensive surveillance and audit trails, building on the regulatory expertise of NYBOT. All conversations with terminal operators are recorded and all keystroke entries made by terminal operators and traders using direct keyboard access are automatically recorded in an electronic audit trail.

- *No price limits or breaks in trading.* Prices appearing on CX are controlled entirely by supply and demand in the market. There are no daily price limits and no circuit breakers to limit trading activity.

The trading platform for both CX and Cantor Fitzgerald's U.S. Treasury cash market is e-speed, one of the most sophisticated and technologically advanced trading systems available. It is capable of processing up to 150 transactions per second and offering customers a variety of options for front-end interfaces. Trading options on U.S. Treasury bond futures is scheduled for mid-2000.

For more information about the Cantor Exchange, contact CX at 212-938-3548 or cx.cantor.com.

Globex

In September 1998, the Chicago Mercantile Exchange (CME) launched its new Globex 2 electronic trading system,

based on NSC technology provided by the French Stock and
Futures Exchanges, the Paris Bourse, and Matif. In February
1999, the CME, the Societe des Bourses Francaises (SBF Baris
Bourse), and the Singapore International Monetary Exchange
(Simex) signed a three-party agreement to begin in the third
quarter of 1999 covering trading in the North American,
European, and Asian time zones using a common electronic
trading platform.

Called the Globex Alliance, the agreement forms a network
of exchanges to offer common access to the broadest range of
derivative products denominated in the world's leading currencies. The alliance gives members of each institution cross-
exchange trading privileges with respect to the others'
electronically traded products, as well as opportunities for cost
savings with cross-margining between products traded at the
exchanges. As part of the agreement, SIMEX will adopt the
NSC electronic trading platform developed by the SBF as its
new electronic trading system, putting all three exchanges on
the same trading platform. The agreement included the two
subsidiaries of the Paris Stock Exchange for futures trading,
Matif SA and Monep SA.

The networks of each exchange are interconnected through
a common interface, also known as a Hub API. The routing and
messaging technology gives exchange members direct access
to the whole range of electronically traded futures and options
offered by the three exchanges. Orders will then be routed to
the appropriate trading engine to be matched and confirmed
back to the member. As a result of the Hub API, independent
software vendors will be able to efficiently connect their front-
end systems to the separate platforms of each exchange
through a single interface.

The Globex Alliance also intends to establish cooperation
on clearing, whereby each clearing house will cross margin interest rate and equity positions with the other two clearing

houses in order to offer members a simple and cost-effective way to reduce capital requirements. Opening a position on a futures or options contract requires a buyer or seller to post a performance bond, or margin, which is determined by the risk of the position. Cross margining provides benefits to "spread" traders who take a position in one market and offset that risk by taking a position in another market. When two contracts are cross-margined, the combined margin required will be reduced if there is a reduction in position risk.

The Globex Alliance also establishes a set of harmonized electronic trading rules and policies, ensuring that traders are not burdened by different sets of policies at each exchange. The agreement calls for the inclusion of additional exchanges with the approval of the three initial parties. The exchanges also have agreed to share in the costs of further enhancements of and modifications to the NSC system.

The CME trades futures and options on futures on agricultural commodities, foreign currencies, interest rates, and stock indexes. The Matif and Monep trade futures and options on interest rates, commodities, stocks, and stock indexes. Simex trades futures and options on interest rates, stock indexes, and energy.

CME also trades two stock indexes electronically: the E-mini S&P and the E-mini Nasdaq. It also offers side by side (open outcry and electronic) trading of Eurodollars futures and options.

E-mini S&P

On September 9, 1997, the CME launched the futures industry's first small-order electronic order routing and execution system for trading the "mini" S&P 500 stock index futures. The "E-mini"—short for electronic mini-S&P—trades on the Globex 2 system and in a high-tech pit, with orders routed in a variety of ways, including the Internet. This land-mark approach allows market participants to harness the most technologically advanced trading and order routing systems in the industry. As a result, it greatly reduces order routing and order execution times. The variety of electronic access medi-ums and the attractive smaller contract size have opened the door to futures trading for many nontraditional futures market participants, such as stock investors.

From day one, the E-mini has been CME's most successful new product. Opening day volume of nearly 8,000 contracts set a record for first day trading, and the E-mini remains the fastest growing index CME has ever launched. To date, aver-age daily volume is more than 17,000 contracts.

An integral component of both Globex 2 and pit execution are electronic order routing systems. CME's own Tops Route system, as well as member firm proprietary order routing sys-tems linked to Tops via CME's order routing API, provides order details to both Globex 2 and the E-mini pit. Member firm account executives, and even customers, are able via a PC to input order details directly into an order routing interface. For all-or-none orders, firms that also interface to Cubs worksta-tions gain additional efficiency. Cubs workstations are located in the pit and are used by brokers to manage order flow and re-port fills. Because the system interfaces with Tops Route, or-ders can be routed entirely electronically, circumventing the need to flash or run orders to pit brokers. Some CME member firms even allow customers to place orders, using their own PCs or computer networks, over the Internet.

The E-mini contracts, sized at one-fifth CME's flagship S&P 500 futures contracts, have attracted a wide range of in-vestors, particularly retail customers for whom the standard contract size is too large. E-mini S&P 500 futures are priced at $50 times the S&P index, or about $48,000 at recent trading levels; the size of each tick is .25 valued at $12.50. Investors can trade the E-mini virtually 24 hours a day. Using the latest in "push" technology, free real-time quotes—not only last price, but valuable bid, offer, and size information—are available on CME's Internet site at www.cme.com under "prices."

E-mini Nasdaq

CME's E-mini Nasdaq contract at $20 times the index is one fifth the regular Nasdaq 100 futures contract. The E-mini Nasdaq provides a very efficient method to manage the risk of the stocks in the index or to participate in this market sector. At recent market levels, the E-mini Nasdaq 100 future contract would be valued at approximately $40,000. The current Nasdaq 100 futures contract has an underlying value at $100 times the index, currently valued at approximately $200,000.

The E-mini Nasdaq 100 contracts trades via a combination of electronic and open-outcry pit trading, paralleling the method that has proven so successful in E-mini S&P 500 futures. The new contracts trade electronically from 3:30 PM until 3:15 PM the following day.

The smaller contracts will be "fungible" with the larger ones, in that positions in the smaller contract may be offset by trading against an equivalent dollar value of standard-size Nasdaq 100 futures and vice versa. A special E-mini Nasdaq 100 "pit," outfitted with Globex 2 screens, has been constructed adjacent to the current Nasdaq 100 pit to accommodate traders on the floor.

The electronic routing system for executing E-mini Nasdaq orders is the same as for the E-mini S&P.

Side-by-Side Trading

Beginning in June 1999, CME introduced side-by-side trading in Eurodollar futures. Increased capability, designed to handle more complex trading strategies and Eurodollar options, will be phased in by January 2000.

The plan calls for installation of dozens of new electronic trading terminals throughout the trading floor, as well as deployment of new hand-held units to enable traders to make markets in both the electronic and open outcry Eurodollar markets from their positions in the pit. The units, which will soon be piloted in the Merc's currency pits, are designed to provide traders with immediate access to the exchange's Globex 2 electronic trading system. The hand-held units also ultimately will provide traders with access to other exchanges and cash markets.

The CME intends to roll out the devices incrementally over the year 2000 with increased capabilities provided.

For more information contact the CME Web site at www.cme.com.

The Theodore Electronic Order Entry System

Theodore is an easy-to-use, Windows NT–based electronic order entry and management system for trading futures and options. It uses state-of-the-art networking technology and features the following:

- A touch-screen interface, designed for speed and ease of use with minimal training

- An integrated suite of customizable workstations for the customer, margin department, order desk (off the floor), order booth (on the floor), and back office.

- Electronically speeds order from customer or broker workstations to the trading floor, reports back fills, and hands off trades to bookkeeping and clearing.

- Supports give-ups and allocation of trades among multiple accounts.

FIGURE 3.1   Theodore Order Entry System

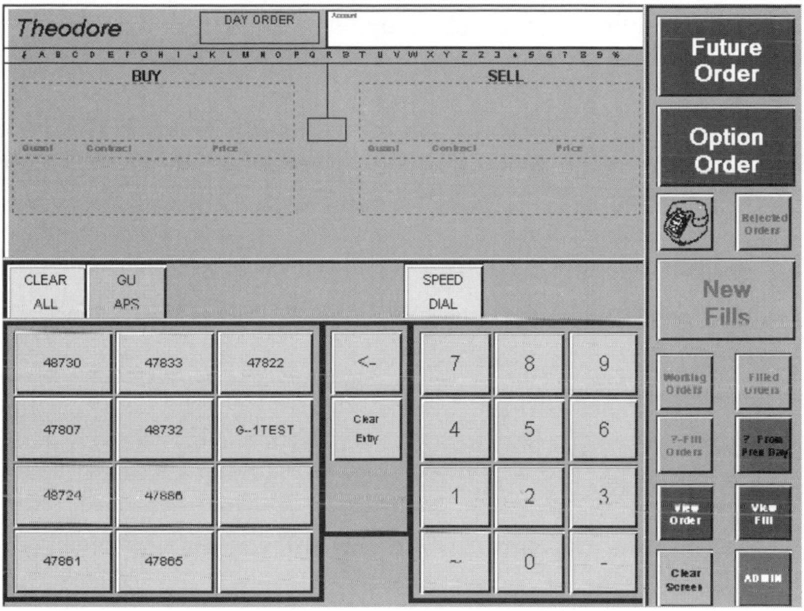

FIGURE 3.2   Theodore Order Entry System

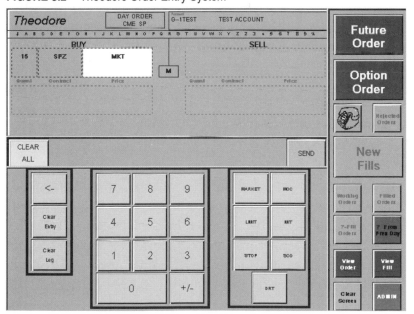

- Modular, scalable architecture using Windows NT platform (client components also support Windows 95).

- Relational database (Microsoft SQL Server) for routing, control, and on-line queries, with continuous availability for up-to-the-second status information on every order and trade, and facilities for full data backup and recovery.

- Industry-standard security features for log-on authentication data access control and encrypted network communications.

- TCP/IP networking links client and server components over a corporate intranet, a public intranet, or dial-up connections.

- Supports off-site monitoring for remote network administration.

- Eliminates dependency on exchange systems, but can interface with them when necessary.

- Supports wireless LAN technology for communications with hand-held units in the pit.

THE INTERNATIONAL SECURITIES EXCHANGE (ISE)

The International Securities Exchange (ISE) will potentially have the greatest impact on electronic options trading for both the hedge and speculative investor. ISE will be the nation's first entirely electronic options market, subject to approval by the SEC. It intends to provide a significantly higher level of efficiency and faster trading for ISE constituents than traditional floor-based exchanges. ISE will provide substantial savings and safeguards for its participants through greatly reduced operating/ transaction costs and the application of market-proven state-of-the-art software technologies and hardware. ISE's mission is to create and maintain an efficient, cost-effective, and liquid market for stock options through the introduction of a new market structure and automated trading systems.

ISE will be an SEC-registered exchange, not an electronic communications network (ECN) or alternative trading system (ATS). A 15-member board of directors, of whom 8 will be nonindustry (public) directors, will provide policy decisions and general direction.

Regulatory Oversight

ISE will be a self-regulatory organization (SRO), registered as a national securities exchange and operating under the oversight of the SEC. As such, ISE has established operating rules designed to provide the public with a fair, orderly, and highly efficient market that gives the highest priority to customer orders. ISE expects SEC approval as a registered exchange before the end of 1999.

As a registered securities exchange, ISE is expected to become a member-owner of and clear its transactions through OCC. As an SEC-regulated exchange and member-owner of OCC, options contracts traded on ISE are fully fungible with the options of the same companies traded on the other options exchanges.

ISE will be the first U.S. market to combine the efficiencies of electronic trading with the time-tested advantages of trading in an open auction market environment. Its goal is to provide a superior market making environment rather than a dealer market, where prices are determined by dealers buying and selling for their own inventory of securities.

ISE's philosophy is that the investing public should be given the highest priority. Thus, its patent-pending trading system has at its core the following:

- Customer orders will be executed before professional orders.

- The price at which a customer order is filled will be the best price available from all options markets; ISE will be the only fully electronic market in the world that incorporates quotes from other exchanges so that customers trade at the best price.

- A complete, detailed electronic record (audit trail) of all transactions, time stamped to the nearest 1/100 of a second, will be immediately available for surveillance purposes.

ISE's combination of electronic trading with auction market principles provides retail investors and professionals with these advantages:

- Significantly reduced cost

- Fast and accurate order execution

- State-of-the-art technology

- Competition in options currently traded on only one exchange

The ISE fee structure will offer the most competitive pricing available for options transactions. This is a direct result of the intense efficiencies inherent to this system. In addition to low exchange charges, there will be no floor brokerage fees for ISE transactions. While firms that employ their own floor brokers do not explicitly pay floor brokerage fees, the cost of memberships and supporting floor brokers and related staff on multiple, traditional exchanges can be substantial.

ISE's system will provide users with an order turnaround time of under one second. This rapid execution and electronic time stamping of orders and quotes, coupled with locked-in trade matching, contributes to the enhanced speed and accuracy of trading on ISE.

All ISE market participants (public investors as well as professionals) will have their orders processed using the same advanced systems. The technology developed by OM Technology for ISE has patents pending on numerous aspects of its groundbreaking functionality. APIs on a variety of user platforms will be provided to allow brokers/dealers to link their order delivery systems to ISE's order management system. In this way, orders from participating brokers/dealers can be routed, executed, and reported electronically with no paper, resulting in significant cost savings. To meet the high-performance needs of ISE, the exchange's platform will be based on Compaq's newest generation of 64-bit Alpha EV6 chip—currently the world's fastest processor.

Competition

Traditional U.S. options exchanges operate with little competition, in that the most actively traded options classes are listed on only one exchange. The SEC has long favored the development of competition in the options market. In 1990 the SEC passed Rule 19c-5 that allowed multiple listing of options; however, no options listed by the markets before that time trade competitively. Of the 600 options most actively traded during 1998, only 42 percent were traded competitively on more than one exchange, while the majority (58 percent) was traded on one exchange only. ISE will provide competition by listing options on 600 of the most widely owned and popular stocks.

OM Technology

OM Technology, the world's leading provider of electronic exchange technology, will provide both ISE's central exchange system and trading stations. ISE will be using an enhanced version of OM's electronic trading system: the OM Click Exchange System. Currently, 13 exchanges around the world have acquired this trading system. It is an open, flexible system based on a client/server environment with an open user interface, which means that a wide range of third-party applications are available for the system.

OM Technology also will supply a highly advanced trading station for market makers on the ISE. This trading station will be based on the technology used in OM Technology's market-leading Orc trading station, an advanced tool for analyzing financial instruments in real time.

OM Technology is part of the Swedish OM Group. OM Technology applies advanced transaction technology to increasing the efficiency of financial and energy markets worldwide. This is done both by developing trading technology and by owning and operating exchanges. The parent company, OM Gruppen, is listed on the OM Stockholm Exchange.

Compaq

ISE's trading software (developed by OM Technology) will operate on Open VMS Alpha Server systems provided by Compaq Computer Corporation. Compaq is the second largest computer company in the world, a Fortune Global 100 company and the primary systems supplier in 106 of the world's 112 exchanges. The Open VMS operating system, Open VMS clusters, and alpha architecture of Compaq provide configuration flexibility, technologies proven in many international markets, and unparalleled growth capacity to handle the high volumes of quotes associated with options trading. Further, this trading system will have multiple redundancies and hot backups.

To fund the formation of ISE, memberships have been sold to a consortium of brokers/dealers organized under the umbrella of Adirondack Trading Partners (ATP) that will provide initial order flow to ISE. The purchase of memberships has provided capital for the development of the trading system, acquisition of hardware, development of regulatory systems, and other costs associated with establishing an exchange. Transaction fees, electronic access fees, and the sale of real-time market data will generate ISE's operating revenues.

ATP's corporate structure and strategy is patterned after Roundtable Partners (Roundtable). Roundtable was organized by a consortium of U.S. brokers/dealers who grouped together to establish two equity market making operations—one for listed securities and one for OTC stocks. Roundtable was so successful after just three years of operation that it went public (in an initial public offering) as Knight/Trimark Group, Inc. In mid-1998, Knight/Trimark ranked number one in volume of the country's OTC market makers. The basis of this success is the collective order flow of the brokers/dealers who were original investors in Roundtable. Unlike equities, there is no third market for options; the creation of an exchange format is the only mechanism by which ATP can replicate the proven model created by Roundtable.

ATP, the consortium of brokers/dealers, accounts for approximately 10 percent (or 130,000 contracts daily) of the total customer order flow in stock options. This order flow provides a solid foundation upon which ISE will build its business. The investors in ATP include Ameritrade; E*TRADE; Herzog, Heine, Geduld, Inc.; Knight/Trimark Group, Inc.; Scottsdale Securities; and other brokers/dealers.

ISE will have three classifications of members, all of whom will be registered broker/dealers.

1. 10 Primary Market Makers (PMM)

2. 100 Competitive Market Makers (CMM)

3. Unlimited number of brokers/dealers who will be Electronic Access Members (EAM)

Primary Market Makers (PMMs)

PMMs will be responsible for maintaining fair and orderly market conditions and continuously providing bid/ask quotations in all their assigned options. PMMs will be required to fill orders at the best available price from among all the competing options exchanges. There will be a total of 10 PMMs assigned the options of up to 60 companies each.

Competitive Market Makers (CMMs)

CMMs will be responsible for maintaining continuous quotations in a smaller group of assigned options than will be required for PMMs. There will be CMMs (initially) for each option.

Electronic Access Members (EAMs)

This group of broker/dealer members will not make markets but will be able to electronically place orders for their customers and proprietary orders for their own accounts. EAMs will pay an annual fee to ISE for access to the exchange. There can be an unlimited number of EAMs.

For more information, contact the International Securities Exchange at www.ISE.com.

CHICAGO BOARD OPTIONS EXCHANGE (CBOE)

In June 1999, the CBOE announced the acceptance of a strategic plan that called for the development of parallel paths in trading technology. Floor-based trading as practiced at CBOE was identified as the preferred method of trading in more actively traded options classes where more than 85 percent of the orders are processed electronically. For these markets, the new technology was seen as a way to enhance its "open outcry" method of trading.

At the same time, CBOE will develop a separate screen-based system to complement floor-based trading. Beginning in 2000, CBOE will begin to move less actively traded stock options to a screen-based trading system. The screen-based system also will be used to facilitate "after hours" trading, which is scheduled to commence in the second quarter of 2000.

Trading Floor Technology at CBOE

As the largest options marketplace in the world, CBOE has emerged as the premier example of technological innovation in the securities industry. The order handling, routing, and execution systems guarantee customers fast and equitable transactions. The CBOE Order Routing System (ORS) is the life-blood of the exchange.

The CBOE ORS currently handles 85 percent of public customer orders. In addition to order routing technology, CBOE has maintained visionary growth on the trading floor. Many market makers that previously used handwritten cards to facilitate trades, now trade with the assistance of 19-ounce hand-held computers. Huge data walls align segments of CBOE's 45,000-square-foot trading floor, providing entire index pits with real-time, dynamic trade data. Reconfigurable display screens (RCN) are abundantly placed in equity trading crowds and display real-time trade data from multiple exchanges.

Retail Automatic Execution System (RAES)

The Retail Automatic Execution System (RAES) was developed by CBOE to provide retail customers with the fastest order executions possible. Orders that fall within designated premium levels, contract size, and series boundaries are guaranteed a fill at the current market bid and offer. This type of order execution system revolutionized trading on CBOE's trading floor. Now, more than 26 percent of public customer orders are executed on RAES.

In most instances, the buy and sell orders submitted by the customer must be 20 options contracts or less, and the premium for the option contract must be below $10. Exceptions include, but are not limited to, options on the Dow Jones Industrial average where up to 50 options contracts are executable on RAES.

Market makers who wish to be eligible to trade incoming orders on RAES must sign on to the system when present in the trading crowd. This is accomplished at several terminals located floor-wide. Once trading begins, the market makers are assigned trades by way of the RAES "wheel." This system randomly selects a letter of the alphabet and assigns the first RAES trade to the corresponding market maker. All RAES executions that follow do so in alphabetical order.

There are two instances where RAES orders cannot be executed automatically. These ineligible orders are referred to as "RAES rejects." The two are:

1. *Reject due to public customer Electronic Order (Ebook).* A RAES trade may be "rejected" due to priority of Ebook. Public customer orders held in Ebook have priority for execution over most other orders. Therefore, if the held order in Ebook "touches" the market bid/offer, but does not trade, then a trade can't be executed on the RAES system either. In most cases, the RAES order would route to another trading system for execution.

2. *Reject due to price competitiveness.* Some options listed at CBOE also may be listed at one or more other exchange(s). A RAES order will not automatically execute at CBOE if another exchange is posting a better quote than CBOE. These orders are printed at the public order book and announced to the trading crowd. The market makers can then contact the other exchange to verify the quote. If they desire they can adjust the CBOE quote and execute the trade.

Public Automated Routing (PAR)

The Public Automated Routing (PAR) system is a PC-based, touch screen, order routing and execution system used by floor brokers. This system allows brokers to easily and efficiently represent a customer order to the trading crowd. PAR has successfully increased the speed at which an order is represented, executed, and filled. This increased speed is attributed to streamlined development of the system. For instance, when a broker selects an order from the workstation, an electronic trading card appears. The electronic card allows the broker to work the order and enter necessary trade information (volume, price, opposing market makers). When the card is complete, the broker can execute the trade with the touch of a finger. Once the broker has submitted the trade, the ORS simultaneously sends a fill report to the customer, and last sale information to the Options Price Reporting Authority (OPRA). OPRA then instantaneously transmits this data to quote vendors worldwide.

PAR is another example of CBOE technological innovation. It reflects the commitment made by CBOE to develop cutting edge trade execution systems. Currently, PAR executes 25 percent of all public customer orders.

CBOE continues to move forward as a technological industry leader with its enhancements to PAR. A successful roll-out of a revised floor broker workstation was recently completed. This innovation equips a floor broker with the ability to facilitate faster and more accurate executions and fill reports. One exciting new feature is the electronic "deck manage," which allows a broker to sort and view all orders on the workstation by specific class. This feature provides a screen where brokers can see all best orders for an entire class on one screen. The broker also is able to view the best bid and offer for each series as well as for the customer's orders listed at the best price. The orders on this screen are color coded to alert the broker to orders that are either away, equal to, or bettering the current market quote.

These competitive advantages were developed to benefit CBOE customers. The new PAR has given floor brokers at CBOE more tools to execute orders in a timely fashion and to report trade information accurately.

Mobile PAR

Wireless initiatives have been integrated into CBOE automated trade execution systems. Independent Floor and Firm Nominee brokers have been equipped with mobile PAR hand-held units to facilitate faster trade executions and fill reporting. This hand-held device is similar in functionality to the stationary PAR workstations. These mobile units bring two specific routing and execution enhancements to the CBOE floor and its customers: (1) firm floor broker and (2) crowd floor broker.

Firm Floor Broker

The introduction of mobile PAR has been a key benefit to member firms, as it enables them to more efficiently manage order flow. When orders route to the booth, they appear on a Booth Automated Routing Terminal (BART) touch screen terminal (more about BART later in the chapter). A clerk in the booth can then select the order and send it to a variety of locations. One of the destinations is a mobile PAR hand-held unit. The mobile PAR enables a floor broker to receive an order, move to the appropriate trading crowd, and execute the order from a mobile PAR order screen. This is all completed by the floor broker without having to return to the firm booth.

Crowd Floor Broker

Crowd floor brokers also have found this new wireless technology to be beneficial in the trading crowd. If a stationary workstation receives heavy volume, the floor broker can designate incoming orders to be routed to additional brokers on the mobile PAR. This adjustment during active trading conditions spreads volume to multiple brokers instead of one individual, which ultimately provides faster order execution and fill reporting to the customer.

Ebook

CBOE provides its customers with a fully automated public customer order book, known as the electronic book (Ebook). Ebook automatically sorts and files orders in price and time sequence. Currently, Ebook executes 31 percent of all public customer orders.

Most orders received prior to the opening of the market are routed to Ebook. This allows a customer order to be immediately represented and, if it is a market order, automatically executed during the opening rotation. Once a market quote is established for an option, ORS will route orders based on price and volume parameters to Ebook.

In addition to being an automated depository for public customer orders away from the market, Ebook gives CBOE staff the ability to manage heavy order flow by adapting the system intraday. CBOE staff can adjust the order flow parameters set by member firms intraday, and route more orders to Ebook in an attempt to ease the burden on floor brokers. Floor brokers also can send all orders from their PAR workstations to Ebook if they become too busy during heavy trading conditions.

Booth Automated Routing Terminal (BART)

The CBOE continued its record of successful innovation with the implementation of BART. BART, also known as the "electronic runner," equips member firms with the ability to better control their order flow. BART allows each firm to customize ORS boundaries (except RAES) to route a certain portion of their order flow to the firm booth. Once these orders reach the booth, they are displayed on a dynamic, PC-based, touch-screen BART workstation. Customer orders then can be electronically forwarded to a destination of the firm's choice.

A firm may elect to route a BART order to a floor broker who can transact business floorwide with a mobile PAR handheld unit. The order would appear on the wireless workstation and the floor broker could execute the order in the proper trading crowd.

Order Routing System (ORS)

A BART operator may desire to send the order back to the exchange's ORS. This could be for two reasons. First, the market may have moved and the order may now be RAES eligible. By sending the order back to ORS, RAES can execute the order and fill report the customer automatically and instantaneously. Second, the order may be away from the current market quote and the firm could deposit the order into Ebook for execution.

Trading Crowd

The firm may elect to route the order to the trading crowd. By pressing the "crowd" key on the workstation, BART will automatically send the order to a PAR workstation of a floor broker in the appropriate trading crowd.

Market Maker Terminal (MMT)

The MMT brings personalized, hand-held computer trading support to market makers on the trading floor. There are currently more than 500 market makers who use the 19-ounce hand-held unit and hand-held trading computers execute approximately 60 percent of all trades floorwide.

MMT provides CBOE market makers with many automated trading advancements. It maintains a market maker's intraday position, providing real-time risk assessment and management to the market maker and the associated clearing firm. The computer also stores all of the option's theoretical values.

One of the most enticing benefits of the MMT is the system's ability to interface with other automated systems:

- *Retail Automatic Execution System Interface.* The MMT interfaces with the RAES system. RAES sends automatic and instantaneous electronic trade acknowledgment to the MMT when a market maker is assigned a trade from the system.

- *Stock Order Routing System.* The MMT interface with this system allows market makers on the CBOE floor to electronically execute stock orders from their hand-held terminals. On October 28, 1997, nearly 8 million shares of stock were bought or sold through this system interface.

- *Electronic Trade Notification* (ETN). ETN is the latest enhancement made to the MMT. An interface has been created between the MMT and other ORS component execution systems. With an ETN, a floor broker and order book official (OBO) can key the trade information into their terminals or workstations, send an ETN with that information to an MMT, and a market maker can either accept or reject the trade. If the trade is accepted, that information is immediately sent on to OPRA and trade match. This process saves market makers time because they no longer need to key trades when trading with Ebook or a broker on a PAR workstation. The system reduces errors because the market maker can check all trade data before it is submitted to trade match.

For more information, contact the Chicago Board Options Exchange at www.cboe.com.

With all these exciting, fast-paced developments taking place in the electronic options trading environment, the sophisticated investor who prepares well both in terms of options training and familiarizing oneself with state-of-the-art software certainly will have a leg up on the competition in identifying and exploiting trading and investment opportunities.

Let's turn now to the actual electronic trading platform to see what it is like to compete on an even playing field with the market makers.

PART TWO

TRADING ON A LEVEL PLAYING FIELD

4

COMPETING WITH MARKET PROFESSIONALS

This chapter presents the essential elements of what you need to know for electronic options trading. Information flow and the ability to respond rapidly to market change is no longer the sole province of the professional options trader. This same opportunity is now open to you.

Options trading is unlike any other kind of trading in that it is dependent on a host of variables: strike price, expiration date, premium, type (call or put), volatility, and the behavior and movement of an underlying instrument. The underlying instrument again can be a stock, bond, index, currency, or commodity. Multiply these elements by a litany of strike prices and you begin to see the challenge of successful options trading.

For the first time, technology has caught up to the demands of the options trader, and it has provided new tools to manage and execute within a large set of dynamic permutations. Risk analysis software has been available for some time and has recently become very sophisticated. What has been lacking until now has been a tool that would combine all the necessary elements of analysis and execution into one package. Some of these important elements are:

- Market windows

- Order entry windows

- Real-time analysis

- Portfolio management

- Risk assessment

- Transaction register

For purposes of illustration, in *The Electronic Trading of Options* we have chosen information from First Traders Analytic Solutions (FTAS), a state-of-the-art options trading software package available spring 2000.

The Market Window

The market window is the most visible of the major components of the software. It is from this basic window that live market quotes are displayed, trades may be executed, and many real-time analyses will be performed. See Figures 4.1 and 4.2.

Order Entry

The trade ticket can be set for expanded or quick key operation. Default settings allow the trader to set up boundaries in advance and execute a trade with the click of a button. See Figures 4.3 to 4.5.

FIGURE 4.1   Market Window

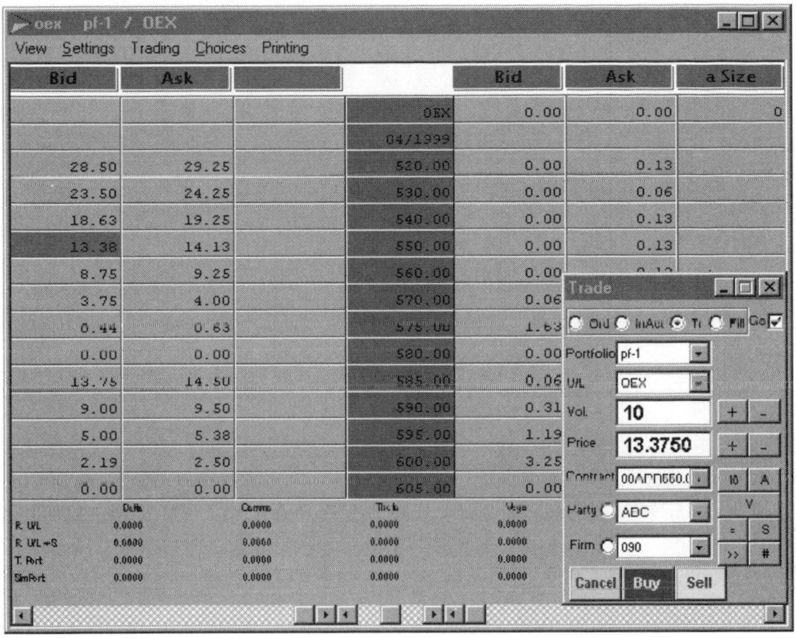

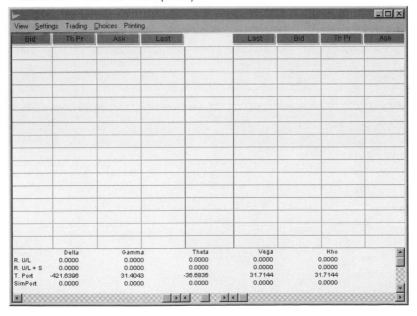

FIGURE 4.2   Market Window (Blank)

FIGURE 4.3   Trade Ticket

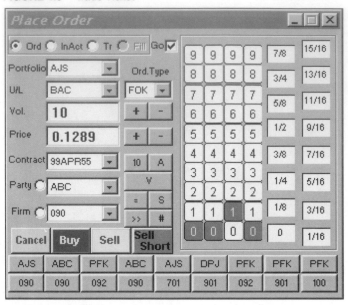

FIGURE 4.4   Bare Bones Trade Ticket

FIGURE 4.5   Expanded Trade Ticket

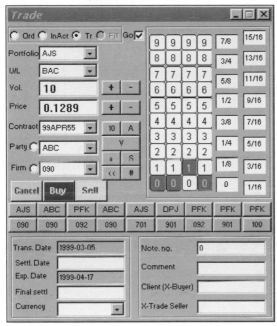

FIGURE 4.6   Real-Time Analysis

```
 Alert List                                                                    _ □ ×
03/05  15:26:48  BUY    CALL  BAC  99MAR 60     @0.00
03/05  15:26:48  BUY    CALL  BAC  99MAR 55     @0.00
03/05  15:26:48  BUY    CALL  BAC  99MAR 50     @0.00
03/05  15:26:48  BUY    CALL  AMGN 99MAR 62.50        @0.00
03/05  15:26:48  BUY    CALL  AMGN 99MAR 62.50        @0.00
03/05  15:26:48  BUY    CALL  AMGN 99MAR 62.50        @0.00
03/05  15:26:48  BUY    CALL  AMGN 99MAR 62.50        @0.00
03/05  15:26:48  BUY    CALL  AMGN 99MAR 60     @0.00
03/05  15:26:48  BUY    CALL  AMGN 99MAR 60     @0.00
03/05  15:26:48  BUY    CALL  AMGN 99MAR 60     @0.00
03/05  15:26:48  BUY    CALL  AMGN 99MAR 60     @0.00
03/05  15:26:12  BUY    CALL  BAC  99MAR 55     @0.00
03/05  15:26:12  BUY    CALL  BAC  99MAR 50     @0.00
03/05  15:26:12  BUY    CALL  AMGN 99MAR 62.50        @0.00
03/05  15:26:12  BUY    CALL  AMGN 99MAR 62.50        @0.00
03/05  15:26:12  BUY    CALL  AMGN 99MAR 62.50        @0.00
03/05  15:26:12  BUY    CALL  AMGN 99MAR 62.50        @0.00
03/05  15:26:12  BUY    CALL  AMGN 99MAR 60     @0.00
03/05  15:26:12  BUY    CALL  AMGN 99MAR 60     @0.00
03/05  15:26:12  BUY    CALL  AMGN 99MAR 60     @0.00
03/05  15:26:12  BUY    CALL  AMGN 99MAR 60     @0.00
```

Real-Time Analysis

This window allows the trader to choose one or several underlying instruments and display market and option model information, all calculated for the most recent market quote. See Figure 4.6.

Portfolio Management

Portfolio management has three major functions: (1) risk identification and management (including all Greeks and real-time risk assessment), (2) position keeping, and (3) results management, which includes considering profit and loss from all trades from the trade ticket. See Figure 4.7.

Risk Assessment

The risk assessment function window calculates the maximum and minimum market value, depending on the risk boundaries: underlying, volatility, interest rate, and time. By redefining these boundaries, a trader can perform simulations and generate the corresponding theoretical values. See Figures 4.8 and 4.9.

Transaction Register

The transaction blotter serves three primary functions. First, it registers all trade and order entries. Second it facilitates trade order management and, third, it functions as an audit and tracking device, which means tracking all changes in trading activity and following all actions to their sources. The transaction blotter, the trade ticket, and the portfolio navigator are completely integrated to facilitate these important functions. See Figure 4.10.

FIGURE 4.7   Portfolio Management

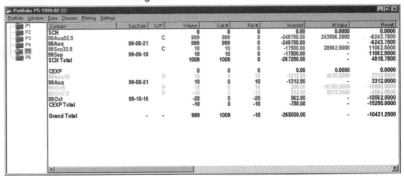

FIGURE 4.8   Risk Assessment

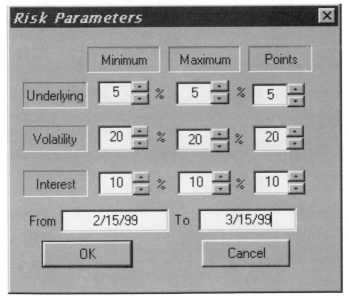

FIGURE 4.9 Risk Report

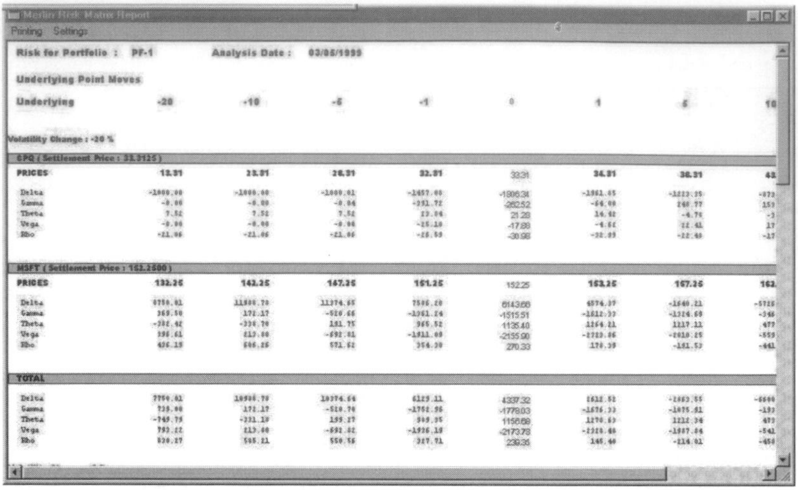

FIGURE 4.10 Transaction Register

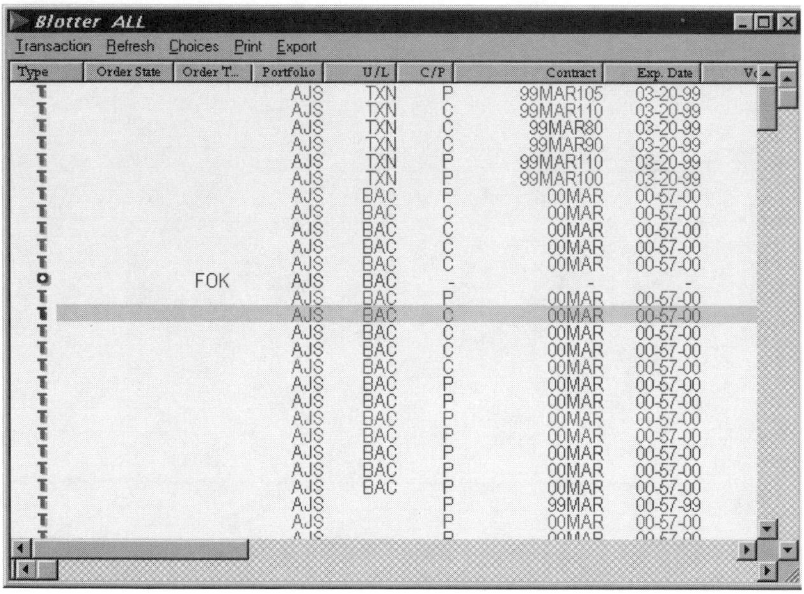

Chapters 5, 6, and 7 are interviews with successful option traders who are currently trading electronically. Joe Corona and Chris Hausman have both been market makers and now trade as part of proprietary trading groups. Tony Saliba probably has more experience with the electronic trading platform than anyone else in the United States. He has set up electronic trading rooms and exchanges (Australia) throughout the world as well as supervises his own team of electronic options traders.

5

INTERVIEW WITH CHRIS HAUSMAN

Chris Hausman is a former market maker and floor trader at the Chicago Board Options Exchange. He is currently an electronic options trader and an instructor on screen-based options trading at International Trading Institute in Chicago. His specialty is equity options.

Q: Chris, what first attracted you to trading?

Chris: Howard, I believe initially it was just the excitement. I was an analyst for an investment bank. I was based out of Dallas at the time. I wasn't all that anxious to spend the rest of my career as a financial analyst working at a desk.

I was lucky. Earlier I had had an internship in the S&P 100 at the Chicago Board Options Exchange (CBOE). So, I was familiar with the floor, but for whatever reason, did not go into trading options right out of college.

Q: When you were a financial analyst, what markets were you analyzing?

Chris: Structured finance, asset backed securities, things like that; typical analyst job coming out of college.

Q: But you were not involved in the trading side of it?

Chris: No, not as an analyst in investment banking. It wasn't until I moved to Chicago that I was involved in trading. I made a decision about six months before I moved so I could prepare myself. I started out by reading every options book that I could get my hands on.

Q: Chris, what attracted you to the options market as opposed to getting involved in securities or in futures?

Chris: Well, I had already been on the floor. That is how I first learned about options trading. Really, just by accident because, as you know, floor trading really isn't something that there's a lot of access or exposure to when you're in school. I mean it's something that the general public really doesn't get to know that much about.

Q: It's not widely known?

Chris: Exactly. So, had I not gotten that internship, I don't know if I ever would have been fully exposed to trading options. I did attend the University of Pennsylvania and as a finance major, I learned about options. So I did have a general exposure to the finance industry and to the options and futures markets.

Q: Chris, could you describe the process of going from your internship to becoming a market maker on the floor?

Chris: I started working for one market maker on the floor of the CBOE and that's where I learned about the different groups that operate on the options trading floor.

Q: Different proprietary traders?

Chris: Proprietary types of groups, sole proprietors, market making firms, brokers, etc. That is how I made the transition from working for a sole proprietor to a market making firm.

Q: Could you talk a little bit about the three different groups that are on the options trading floor, because our readers may not be familiar with them.

Chris: Well, first there's the sole proprietors. These are people who have capital and trade for themselves. There are arbitrage groups where the traders trade for a common goal. They use the firm's capital, but they're not individual option traders and they are trading a single plan or strategy for a common objective. There are also firms who back people, who are in the business of lending out capital so that traders can trade for their own accounts with the firm taking a percentage of profits. Those are the three main types of groups that you'll find. Most everyone on the floor who is trading will fall into one of those categories.

Q: What kind of market maker were you?

Chris: I worked for an arbitrage group; I was part of an options trading team. I felt that starting out on the floor, I would have the best exposure to many different traders and trading styles this way. I felt this experience would help to shape my trading down the road.

Q: Chris, could you describe what it is like to be part of an arbitrage team; what are some of the responsibilities of the different players and what were the overall goals of your group? Also, how did you work at optimizing your trading performance?

Chris: Well, the most important thing is always information. What was happening in my trading pit was affected by what was happening in all the other pits our group was involved in. I was trading in the S&P 500 options pit at the Chicago Mercantile Exchange (CME). It was very important to know what was going on in the other pits—communication for an arbitrage group is key! The other team members were trading options at the CBOE where we could lay off the risk.

So we were basically performing arbitrage in the pits. Howard, I think going back to your original question about what attracted me to options trading is their versatility. As long as you learn how to trade options, you can apply trading strategies and principles to any underlying product, whether it is a foreign currency or an index or a security. That was the key for me. I never came out and specifically said to myself, "I want to trade options in stocks, currencies, or fixed income." Once you learn how to trade options, you can step into any one of those arenas and trade.

Q: So it is the versatility of the option, meaning that the option gives you the ability to lay off risk in a number of different ways. Are you saying that is what attracted you to options and your method of approaching the market?

Chris: Exactly. It wasn't the underlying product. As far as I was always concerned, the underlying product was my hedge and nothing else. It didn't matter if it was a commodity, security, bond, or index.

Q: So, your trading judgments initially were based on your ability to hedge risk, is that it?

Chris: Right, based on option pricing. But remember, everyone has different risk tolerances.

Q: Could you describe what your experience was like as a market maker? Exactly what were you doing and what were your goals on a day-to-day basis?

Chris: On the trading floor your main objective is volume. With options trading, the more volume you do, the more edge you capture in the long run. So, it requires you to be as active (vocal) as possible. And being in the physical trading pit, your voice and your presence is one of the major components of your trading. I mean you have to get the broker's attention to get the trade! You have to have a high level of energy throughout the day; especially when news comes out or the market is extremely whippy at high volatile times. You're constantly focusing on order flow. Trading in this way requires speed and fast reaction.

Q: Chris, when you were working on the trading floor, did you find that you were trying to execute specific option trading strategies or were you more focused on capturing edge?

Chris: I was definitely more into capturing the edge. I wasn't really putting on positions with an opinion of market direction. However, I would put on positions based on volatility. I would usually take an opinion on volatility and position myself accordingly. Using strategies that are based on volatility plays.

Q: Can you elaborate on the concept of volatility and how you would use it?

Chris: Well, I would look at the volatility between different spreads. Trying to buy volatility when it was low, and sell volatility when it was high. Just knowing how volatility acts when the underlying product is rallying or when it's breaking. I mean, there's different types of volatility. Volatility acts in certain ways. You have to prepare yourself or insulate yourself for these different scenarios. I may not have cared if the stock went up or down, but I definitely knew what was going to happen to the volatility if the stock moved sharply one way or the other. And having in my trading toolbox the ability to adjust positions to changing market conditions.

Q: To massage the volatility?

Chris: Yes. To know how to use it to my overall advantage.

Q: Can you discuss how electronic trading has changed your overall style or strategy of options trading?

Chris: Well, I think upstairs in front of a screen the edge component of trading is no longer there. You have to do more analysis, and have more of an opinion regarding the stock or other underlying product in terms of what kind of strategies to use. I'm still following volatility. It's probably my main thing. But there's also more risk/reward in my strategies, where I'm trying to gain the maximum in volatility for the amount of risk that I'm willing to take. And that is based for the most part from stock to stock on how each has moved in the past. Simply stated, it's the movement of the stock and the magnitude of the volatility and the way the options are priced that we're constantly looking at. Everything else, everybody knows and all the other inputs in a model are known.

Q: Can you elaborate on that, when you say movement of the stock and the volatility?

Chris: I mean the movement of the stock is going to create the volatility. Whether it's going up or down will dictate the volatility of options. In the simplest sense, volatility is how the supply and demand responds.

Q: Do you both buy and sell volatility?

Chris: What you want to do is buy low and sell high. You want to buy cheap volatility and sell high volatility. At some point the marketplace will reverse itself as it relates to volatility pricing.

Q: How do you determine whether the volatility is high or low?

Chris: Historical volatility would be the best. It obviously doesn't predict the future. But it's one way to get an opinion on when we're low and when we're high.

There are two types of volatility: implied volatility and historical volatility. Historical volatility refers to the changes that have been noticed over time in the marketplace. An implied volatility is a quantitative number that is disseminated through the option prices. A basic option-pricing model gives you theoretical value of your options, with volatility being one of the inputs. If you don't know what volatility is, then take the option prices that the market is disseminating and enter those into the model to determine the volatility. In essence, that is implied volatility.

Q: So, do you rely more on historical or implied volatility?

Chris: Historical to get a sense of where the market could go. The implieds again follow a mathematical rule based on probabilities that have to be followed. So day to day, we are following the implieds but smoothed out. Unfortunately, there are kinks. Not all the markets disseminated are well priced in terms of being quoted. They may be a half or a quarter of a point out of line, and looking at the implieds and comparing them to a smooth volatility curve that is mathematically correct allows you to take advantage of some significant arbitrage opportunities.

Q: Chris, could you talk about your experience with electronic trading because now you're trading options primarily on a screen. What was your learning curve in terms of developing facility on an electronic trading platform?

Chris: I'm of the generation that grew up with Nintendo and computers. Being an electronic trader for me was just an invitation! I've done a lot of research and reading on the European markets and the Sydney Exchange and I believe it's just a matter of time before all options trading goes electronic. I think it's inevitable. Especially now with the advent of the International Securities Exchange (ISE), which is a fully automated, electronic options trading exchange.

I guess my feelings for moving off the floor was based on the technological changes I saw occurring and my belief there were more to come. It was time to learn the electronic platform and adapt my style of trading

Q: Chris, you mentioned the ISE. Could you talk a little more about what you think is the future of options trading?

Chris: It will definitely depend on how the ISE does. I mean hopefully it will do well. Frankly, I don't see why all option trading won't go electronic. Of course, there's always the argument that the pit provides liquidity in times of volatility. You know, that was fine when trading systems couldn't handle a billion shares on the New York Stock Exchange, but today they're handling a billion shares a day with nobody blinking! So, I think the argument of machines never replacing human beings because of liquidity isn't persuasive. There are still human beings behind the screens!

Are they going to back off and just watch the screen when the market gets volatile? I doubt it. There always will be players in search of opportunities. The beautiful thing about volatility is everyone has a different opinion about it. What I think is high, someone else may think is low. In essence, that's what creates a marketplace. If we all had the same opinion, if everyone had the same theoretical value, nobody would ever be trading!

Q: What do you think are the specific tactical demands of electronic trading that makes it different from open outcry?

Chris: With screen-based trading, there is not the social pressure that there is in a pit. When you are looking for a certain edge, I think the market's also going to be tighter, as they are in Europe with one- and two-tick wide markets. The traders who are going to be able to do more size and settle for less edge are the ones who are going to be sticking around. For this reason, I believe the trader who is a sole proprietor on the floor today will have a harder time competing against the firm-based trader. Institutional traders have more resources and more capital.

Q: Could you walk me through your trading day in front of the screen? Tell me what you're doing day to day at the most fundamental level: how you're focusing on the bid and ask, how you're looking at your theoretical models of value, and how you determine whether there is a trade to take or one to avoid?

Chris: To begin with, I'm always analyzing my book, meaning my inventory. So, I have a position which has certain risk characteristics. Once I put on a position with edge, how do I take it off profitably? How do I get in and get out and capture this edge to theoretical value? This is the analysis I am constantly doing: analyzing how my profit and loss are going to suffer or gain according to where the stock is, given different volatility parameters. So, I'm constantly analyzing risks, constantly figuring out exactly where I am or where I could be: running different trades in my mind under different market scenarios.

Q: Run through a couple of them with me, Chris, just so the reader gets a sense of what you're thinking and what the mental process is while you're trading.

Chris: Sure. Let's take for example a down move. Down moves historically have been larger than up moves and they've been faster. It's not a great secret that with down moves, volatility increases. So, I would definitely be aware of where the underlying product is and have some type of control in place to monitor how fast volatility could increase on a down move. I would take into account the size of the move and how fast it happened. I would have a sense of how quickly the volatility would rise.

Q: So, if you're seeing the potentiality of a large down draft in the market, you're looking to buy volatility, is that it?

Chris: Yes, to take advantage of the gamma, because hopefully the move will mean volatility will increase and then the gamma movement will also be advantageous in my position. And conversely, if I have the opposite position, that is, I need volatility in my book, now's the time to really cover my position; otherwise my inventory is going to suffer. So, it's kind of constantly analyzing my risk and exploiting or covering accordingly.

Q: What do you believe is the role of technical analysis for the electronic options trader?

Chris: I think technical analysis, as far as understanding the movement and price action of the underlying product, is important. I don't really know of any specific viable technical analysis for the options in and of themselves. If there was a way to develop some technical analysis for volatility, I think that would be useful for us.

Q: Chris, I was specifically speaking about the underlying product, in terms of getting a sense of the direction or market action, in order to form a judgment about the best options strategy to use to take advantage of an opportunity.

Chris: Well, with technical analysis, it is obviously important to form an opinion of whether a stock is going to go up or down. And once you have that worked out, there are a myriad of options strategies that you can create to address whether the stock is going to go up, go down, or stay in a range.

Q: Does that form the basis of your judgment, like when you're taking a position? Are you using pattern recognition or momentum indicators?

Chris: Usually momentum, because we're focused on trading the volatility. We're trying to predict where the volatility could be next. Momentum would be my best indicator so that I can apply the proper options strategy.

Q: So, if there's one thing you're looking at more than anything else, it is volatility?

Chris: That's right. I'd like to mention one other thing. Another key reason for my going electronic was the ability to trade different products or stocks. Being in one pit makes it difficult to trade other things. Now I have the ability and opportunity to trade many different options on equities. And the other thing is there's also cross border trading. Now, with Eurex, I'm going to have the ability to trade Europe. If you're not on an electronic platform, that opportunity is not there for you.

Q: Chris, how many different stocks are you trading on any given day?

Chris: Usually I trade anywhere from 5 to 15, and I'm looking to move up. You obviously want to trade stocks that have volume.

Q: What are some of the names you trade on a daily basis?

Chris: AOL, IBM, Yahoo, Amazon. Right now the Internet sector is a player, so that attracts a lot of options traders. And with all the movement, there is a lot to do as a savvy options trader. Also, as a volatility trader, it's the best type of stock for me to trade. With so much movement, the volatility is up, then it's down, I couldn't ask for a better type of stock to trade.

Q: I guess when trading these names, a trader certainly needs to be disciplined in his or her approach to the market. Could you talk a little bit about what you think is the role of psychology for being a successful trader?

Chris: The discipline comes with knowing how to hedge yourself. I think that is the number one thing for an options trader.

Q: Hedging your risk?

Chris: Yes, hedging your delta risk.

Q: Are you always trying to trade close to delta neutral?

Chris: Yes, excessive delta risk could wipe out any volatility gain or any gamma gain instantly. So, the number one hedge is your delta: I go to the underlying stock to do that. However, sometimes the stock moves by the time you've done your options trade and then you go to your stock but the stock has moved.

Q: Chris, what you are saying then is at times it may look like you have a big edge in the options market, but that would be contingent on being able to trade the underlying product at a specific price, right? Then you find you don't have that price available to you.

Chris: Right. I mean we're using relative pricing when we do our options. And knowing where you get your stock price is part of that equation. So, if the stock price isn't there where you value your option price, then it could be a negative edge or a negative scalp! So, at that point you have a decision to make. You have a naked option and your decision comes down to this: At what point do you just hedge the stock and basically from a theoretical perspective make the option a loser? That's why I do use technical analysis when I miss buying the stock, to determine where the breakouts are going to be.

Q: It sounds almost as if you use technical analysis defensively, meaning that if you can't buy the underlying exactly where you need to hedge your delta, you use technical analysis to determine your safety zone.

Chris: Yes, that's right. When I was in the pit, you could definitely see where a breakout would be. If I was hung—

Q: Hung, meaning you owned the options but hadn't covered the underlying?

Chris: Yes. I would immediately view the chart and act accordingly. I think technical analysis used proactively could be an enormous asset to options traders who take on a directional play.

Q: Chris I would like to return to the subject of psychology. What do you think are the common characteristics of successful options traders?

Chris: I think discipline is the first. Discipline in the sense that you always have to analyze where you're at. What are your risks and what is your personal risk threshold?

Q: You had mentioned earlier that embracing risk is a subjective thing.

Chris: Every trader must know how much money he or she is willing to lose. Some people give a dollar amount. When I was floor trading, I would give myself a dollar amount to lose before I would just cover it and then move on. Some people gave percentage amounts. It's dependent on one's own subjective risk parameters.

Q: How do you do it now?

Chris: Howard, it's not an exact science. I think it's based on how much I know I can make in a day.

Q: And it's some percentage of that?

Chris: Yes. Some percentage of that that I'm willing to lose. And then, when I'm having a good day, that percentage naturally increases. But, it still always comes down to the trading axioms: Let your winners run and cut your losers short. Easily said, but one of the hardest things to do!

Q: Chris, as an instructor, what are some of the obstacles that you see new electronic options traders facing?

Chris: I think the first obstacle is just the confidence issue. You know, you start trading on a powerful electronic platform and you are competing against traders who have been around for years. It comes down to getting the best possible preparation, having the best trading tools, and really believing in yourself. Ultimately, you must rely on your skills. That's what we teach here. Each trader possesses knowledge of a lot of different spreads and a lot of different types of strategies for different market scenarios. Traders learn how to get in and how to get out. And how to recognize when they shouldn't be trading.

Q: Do you find novice traders are more prone to using specific strategies and to what extent are those strategies ultimately inhibiting to their overall performance?

Chris: Obviously, novice traders are going to be aware of only a few different types of strategies, a few different types of spreads, which are only good under specific scenarios. The great thing about options is you can create any type of spread, if you can imagine it. That's the versatility with electronic options trading. The more spreads you know and the more tools you possess allow you to understand how the risk intertwines with other strike prices. There isn't a single scenario that can't be addressed with a specific options strategy. You are constantly changing with a market that is dynamic. For example, let's take a volatility opinion. If you think the stock is going to stay right where it is, you may use a butterfly spread. You can go long or short volatility, using different types of butterfly spreads. Or, if you really have a huge opinion on volatility or directional bias, you may opt for a straddle or strangle (fully explained in Chapter 2). Those are some of the basic spreads that you can do. There are strategies that will profit in an up or down move or no move. It really comes down to how you want to package it, as they say, and what you think of the underlying stock, commodity, currency, bond, or index.

Q: Chris, what words of advice would you offer to someone who is planning to become an electronic options trader or someone who has just begun trading options?

Chris: I think education is the key. You want to be able to go down and screen-base trade with as many types of strategies underneath your belt or in your toolbox as possible. The more you know, the better off you're going to be; the more you're going to be able to see market opportunities. In turn, that's going to lead to more arbitrage opportunities for you as well.

Q: Chris, let's speak now about TradeStar, and perhaps you may want to talk about how electronic options traders can benefit from using it?

Chris: I believe TradeStar is the best screen-based educational trading tool available. It teaches traders first of all options pricing. It teaches traders how to value options without having theoretical value based on call and put prices.

Just 15 years ago, professional market makers didn't have theoretical values. Well, how did they trade? They did it by relative value pricing and that's what traders learn on TradeStar. As you go on, it gives you different scenarios, for example, volatility scenarios. And it penalizes you if you go outside of circumscribed risk/reward parameters. It teaches market discipline and profitable trading in a very specific and concrete way. It also mirrors the electronic screen that market makers use. I think as we approach 2000, enormous opportunities will be opening up for electronic options traders. There is Eurex, ISE, CBOE, Globex, and Liffe Connect. The age of electronic options trading is here.

6

INTERVIEW WITH TONY SALIBA

Anthony J. Saliba has been a pioneer and active participant in the Chicago derivatives markets for nearly 20 years. He holds exchange memberships on the Chicago Board Options Exchange (serving on the Board of Directors from 1987–1989), The Chicago Board of Trade, and the Chicago Mercantile Exchange.

Q: Tony, how would you characterize the transition from trading on the floor, which is essentially open outcry, to screen-based options trading?

Tony: Some of the skill set components are completely transferable and others are just a fond memory! The technicals and the ability to analyze your positions and to determine proper volatility levels for pricing, your hedging methodologies, your view of the marketplace in general, all those transfer 100 percent. In fact, they'll be enhanced acutely due to the fact you'll have more automation and more technological tools to assist you, right at your fingertips.

In terms of response time and identification of opportunities, that is, capturing order flow, which is a key component of being part of the crowd where your focal point is watching the "paper" (buy and sell orders) come in . . . that changes dramatically. When you are part of the crowd, you are alerted to trades by the reaction of other traders or a broker trying to catch your attention. Technology will assist you in that respect, in terms of

95

identifying opportunities, but it will not be as concentrated. Of course, the software you end up trading with also is key.

Q: Tony, could you talk in personal terms about what it was like for you moving from trading options on the floor to trading electronically on a screen?

Tony: Although on the trading floor there are many different types of traders, each of them, to some degree, must be a market maker. They also must contribute pricing in series that they don't necessarily want to.

Now, trading electronically is completely different. Upstairs you have the ability to be completely a buyer if you want. You can now be a price taker as opposed to a price maker or a market maker. You have a potpourri of prices from which to check that are also orders in a sense, because they're backed by depth and quantity. And I'm talking strictly from personal experience, the first time you get in front of a screen, you're almost like a kid in a candy store. "Wow," you say to yourself, "they'll trade at those prices?" And not necessarily all the prices are theoretically profitable prices for you! But when you're standing in a crowd, you just can't turn to the other guy as you well know and say, "Oh, Howard, I'll sell you a hundred on your bid." When you're trading electronically, the anonymity allows you to just go crazy if you are not disciplined.

What you'll find in talking to some of the other electronic traders is that you could overtrade very easily.

Q: Overtrade just because there's so many different markets and bids and offers available to you?

Tony: Yes, I started trading the German stocks. You had markets where all of the strikes had reasonable depth and reasonable width, and consequently it was easy to get yourself in trouble and overtrade.

Q: Did you find yourself overtrading?

Tony: Yes, particularly in the futures, in the underlying. Well, I just bought some here, a painless click, and when they went lower, I would buy a few more, another painless click. You don't have someone yelling in your face, as you do on the trading floor, which is sort of a subconscious reminder that maybe you should rethink what you are doing.

Q: Electronic trading is sort of a bloodless and sweatless trade, right?

Tony: Yes. It's the same thing with trading stocks; it's easy to fall into that same problem. But with options, it was exaggerated because never before could I just have all the bids and asks at my fingertips to buy and sell whenever I wanted.

Q: Tony, how did you get over the tendency to overtrade?

Tony: Fortunately I had some very good resolve and discipline. And in talking to my friends who are electronic traders, I found they were having the same problems or could fall into that situation of overtrading if they weren't careful. So, what I have done is incorporate into our options training program guidelines for traders to stay in acceptable risk parameters; with strong emphasis on not crossing those lines.

Q: So, the point is that by developing highly defined objective risk analysis software, you tamed your natural inclination to overtrade?

Tony: Right. That's what I did for my employees. For me personally, I mean believe me, it was quite easy to accumulate huge positions by a mouse click. And I'd just say to myself, "Boy, I've got a lot of risk here!" Normally I would have to work fairly hard on the trading floor to accumulate that kind of risk. So, I was just fortunate that I had enough internal resolve, plus I developed an objective risk analysis software that I could refer to.

Q: Tony, let's talk about some of the specific electronic trading platforms that will soon revolutionize options trading: specifically Eurex, Globex, Liffe Connect, ISE, and CBOE.

Tony: Eurex is the granddaddy of the platforms. The Eurex system was built between 1985 and 1986 by Arthur Andersen on a UNIX platform that is digitally based, with VMS software. It was launched by Sofex, the Swedish Options and Financial Features Exchange, in the summer of 1987. That platform then migrated. The Swiss and Arthur Andersen sold it to the Germans—that is, to the DTB—which became Eurex in '88. They made some modifications. It is still quite a bit true to the original platform in that the order matching and the mainframe software are 14 years old. But in fairness, they have made some great changes. They've developed a front end with multiple flavors. You can use a UNIX front end or a Windows NT front end. They also have a very open platform now. When it comes down to trading options, your front end is really important. It is basically the name of the game when trading options electronically. If you're on a rotten system that is closed, you're going to confront some serious problems. But the DTB—now Eurex—has kept pace with the needs of the marketplace to a great degree—more so in the last two or three years, by making the system open.

Today there are quite a few third-party vendors. So the end user has flexibility to have software to do the things that he or she wants to do. In the early days, you could only do what the exchange's system did. In general, I would say that Eurex is pretty much state of the art.

Q: But it's not currently available to the average investor?
Tony: No, not right now. The Eurex platform is unlike stock trading where you get an ECN and it is linked to other

ECNs and then to the New York market—so all of a sudden you have a confluence of all of the U.S. systems being connected together. The options systems currently are unique to the product that they're licensed to trade. Each system is like its own little country. And so, right now, Eurex has a specific product base. But in a year or two, this all could be very different because electronic platforms build markets. There is a natural progression to all of these electronic trading platforms in terms of how widely they are distributed. At first, the exchanges start out by asking if they can just put their "box" out with their own products. Then they seek partnerships with other exchanges, offering products with more features and use of their box. The next step may be mutual listings of products. Eventually the system will become part of the public domain. I think it is inevitable.

Q: Do you see a time, Tony, when people will be able to trade Eurex the same way they might trade on a Nasdaq level 2 today?

Tony: Yes. But I don't think the speed of the change will be as fast as it has happened with electronic stock trading. First, the SEC is totally behind ECNs and the proliferation of stock trading in the U.S. Second, Eurex is a foreign entity and not viewed with the same degree of priority by the governing agencies.

It took two years just to get a no action letter from the CFTC, which allows Eurex to distribute their boxes with their products on our turf. So, I believe the adoption of Eurex will be slower and more methodical. Also, the fact that their products are derivatives with different risk characteristics than stocks engenders a more watchful eye.

Q: What about Globex?

Tony: Globex is more in line with a Eurex style trading platform. It is a full and complete system. Globex is an evolution of a couple of different systems, the Reuters System and now the Securite Bourse Francais (SBF).

Q: Do you think as time goes on that Globex will be more widely available to options investors?

Tony: I think so. I certainly think it can be. I think the goal of the MERC (Chicago Mercantile Exchange) is to first have it succeed with the professional trader. It's the same with Eurex. Their terminals currently aren't in the hands of the end user. It's not reached the same level of a SOES trading room or a Nasdaq level 2 screen traded at home off a PC. But there is no reason options trading can't soon be at that point.

Q: In Europe today, a customer who wants to trade Eurex is sending in an options order like a retail customer would at an E-Schwab or Suretrade. Is that correct?

Tony: Right, or he's first sending it to a brokerage house that then routes it electronically. Liffe Connect is also similar to Eurex and Globex, but of course trading a distinct product line. Globex, Eurex, and Liffe Connect are all in the same category in terms of their platforms. Another platform is based on OM (Options Market Sweden) technology. Today OM Sweden trades all Swedish and some Norwegian products, along with products in about seven other countries. This is the technology of the ISE.

Q: Primarily equities?

Tony: No, they trade everything. They're pretty much of a potpourri of equities, pulp products, currencies, fixed income, and OTC products. They're very innovative. In fact, they initially started with a phone and white board marketplace in the late '80s and beat out the open outcry market. Initially, OM was a telephonic exchange. Market makers would call in their bids and offers and then a quote reporter would put them up on something like a Reuters terminal. It was completely transparent. Everybody could see the market from his or her terminal. That was actually the beginning of the OM system. And then they migrated from the telephonic market to their existing electronic platform, which is probably the most open state-of-the-art system in use at the present time.

Q: Is OM available to the general investor?

Tony: That's decided on a case by case basis with each exchange in every country. Their platform is used in Finland, Austria, Hong Kong, Norway, and Australia. I think they're working on Canada. But currently you must be a licensed broker dealer to take advantage of their direct electronic access. Now, with the introduction of the ISE, I think that will change everything.

Howard, let's establish that there are three levels of end users. The first is the pro, there to make markets. In other countries, these mostly work for banks and brokers. Often it is someone who has migrated off the trading floor and all he does all day is make markets. The second level is the price taker, someone who wants the same level of professionalism and direct access as the first, but not necessarily the obligation to make markets. And then there is a third level and that would be your retail end user. He or she is a casual or not so casual user of the product, someone who would like to skip going through a broker and having that terminal for individual investment use.

Q: For the most part, Tony, that third layer at this point in time does not have entry into the systems we have been discussing.

Tony: No, but it is inevitable that he or she will soon have that access, particularly with the introduction of ISE. I'd say by the end of 2000. ISE stands for International Securities Exchange. Their first listed group of products is to be options on the top 600 most liquid U.S. stocks. It is a U.S.-based exchange set up by American market professionals from the stock and options business. ISE will also have the benefit of OM technology. So ISE has strong capital backing from market participants with seasoned players both on the administrative and operational levels. They've got a service provider that is experienced and a hardware distributor (Compaq) that is formidable.

Q: Tony, do you think ultimately ISE will have an electronic trading system that will be comparable in the near term to a Nasdaq level 2; where a trader will be able to bang out option prices, take a look at volatility, and compete with the market makers on listed U.S. equity options?

Tony: Yes, I do, but it'll be in stages. And I think it would be a mistake to make it available on too broad a basis too soon. Because they need to have content. You see we would all welcome that level of direct market access. All traders want to be market takers; we want to hit the bid if we need to. We want to do our own thing. And the big difference is the obligation to make markets. So, ISE currently needs to build a base of market makers to provide bids and offers with depth. You already have had that with Nasdaq for 20 years. Nasdaq level 2 has been a natural progression.

ISE has got to build that base first. And that isn't going to happen in a month or two. It's going to take some time. If they're real successful it could happen in six to nine months where they can establish strong markets. At that point it will make sense to open it up to the next level and let the retail investor trade electronically direct.

Honestly, I think you're talking about a year to two-year period, at best, for that to happen. And I could be completely wrong. It may happen faster; but I think their market would get diluted too quickly if they don't build content initially. You know, Howard, we also need to talk about CBOE's system because it currently provides a viable electronic platform to the electronic investor. CBOE is currently close to 90 percent electronic in its order routing and matching.

Except for the fact that there is some human interface when the order comes to the crowd, it is by and large paperless. Orders are transmitted to the point where they virtually match electronically. The only difference here from a purely electronic platform is that there is a human aspect that is still maintained. And that has to do with giving the crowd a chance to better the market and then the order is back into the cyberworld.

So, in reality, the CBOE could introduce electronically direct, level 2–like trading to the end user a little faster because it already has that critical mass. They have proposed side by side electronic trading currently in liquid markets, and all electronic trading in some of the more illiquid options markets. ISE, on the other hand, does not, I believe, have the ability to bring a level 2–like system to the marketplace now.

They couldn't roll out a level 2–like platform to a retail end user because they don't have that critical mass. CBOE has the critical mass, but it doesn't have the proven screen-based technology yet. So, it'll be a foot race here. CBOE is going to bring out its screen-based technology before the end of the year in an effort to preempt ISE.

If it sees at that point that its technology works, then it can offer direct trading across the board because it already has the bids and asks. It already has the marketplace, the critical mass to piggyback upon. I believe that it could build on itself tremendously! CBOE could blow everybody away. It's a big gamble though because if its software doesn't come through, then nobody's going to want to use it. But CBOE is spending a lot of time and money on it. It's a great effort!

I'm betting that it will work; that it's going to be successful right out of the box—plug and play! That the market will use it straight away.

Q: Tony, when do you see it in operation for all investors?

Tony: The second quarter of 2000. Like I said, I think if CBOE hits its stride, it could be providing electronically direct options trading before ISE because it has the critical mass to do so. It's already exploring how to do this online, where you as an online trader can get depth and some accountability. It's trying to determine what kind of secure Web site access is required for the end user.

I think the opportunities that will open up to options traders on all three of the levels I discussed before will be tremendous. The electronic trading platform will be in place. The key is going to be knowledge and training.

Q: Tony, you have worked with more than 100 electronic trading desks in seven or eight countries around the world. You have your own successful group of proprietary options traders. From your perspective, where does the market savvy investor get his or her edge? And how have you built that into your electronic simulator, TradeStar?

Tony: Howard, first of all ITI has trained nearly 5000 professional market makers and brokers. TradeStar is geared to state-of-the-art electronic trading; trading that is screen based and designed to teach traders at all levels to compete successfully.

To a large degree, trading is about familiarity with rhythms, that is, visual and audio cues. There's definitely a style and a rhythm that the trader can get into where he or she eliminates all extraneous information that is detrimental to them. The training style we use is a combination of lecture and lab. What TradeStar accomplishes and what the training develops, is a highly-trained, sophisticated, screen-based electronic options trader.

Unlike stock trading, which is by and large one dimensional, options trading is complex and requires a thorough grounding in theory. That is why we concentrate so heavily on basic strategy:

pricing, volatility, risk analysis, and knowing how to break down a position. We take all this and then superimpose it on the game, on the actual practical functioning of the marketplace where prices are changing. Colors on the screen are changing, relationships are changing. And when they change in such a way that provides an edge for you or an opportunity or an entry point, we teach you how to recognize them and react and do it repetitively in order to be profitable. So, our training helps somebody get an edge by eliminating a lot of the "noise" in the market and understanding what is essential: How to operate using these strategies and superimpose them onto a state-of-the-art electronic trading platform.

Q: Tony, based on your long experience with traders and trading, what would you say makes for a successful options trader in general, and a successful electronics options trader in particular?

Tony: I'd say they require basically the same skills: There's instinct, mathematical skills, and creativity in managing volatility, as well as quick and decisive reactive skills.

Q: Mathematical skills in terms of knowing the relationship between the underlying and the different strikes?

Tony: Yes, and to some degree understanding how the models work. You'll be able to determine how much edge is required in certain series versus how much edge is required in other series. Quarter edge across the board isn't an equal quarter edge. Mathematical skills in terms of being able to quickly make the comparisons and make the relationship judgments. Also, you have to work with your tools, so that you can derive the right responses. It's important to understand mathematics in that respect. Most team traders upstairs have a quantitative department so a lot of them don't have to worry about that. But, there's also the level of tolerance and the ability to know when you bought too much at a level to bring it on down or you sold too much at a level and start to bring it up. You have to feel when to press and when to back off. There's some personal skill sets, mathematical skill sets, and, as I said a moment ago, creativity.

Q: Sounds like art and science.

Tony: Correct. It's a skill set of both. We always said here in my shop that trading options is both an art and a science. The science will not always win out without the art. And without the science, art will just get you in trouble.

Q: Does that change on an electronic platform?

Tony: It does. It's a great question because it does change a situation where a guy who wasn't so mathematically sound in the past now has new tools available to him. He's in a cockpit. He's got software. He's got analytics now that if used properly with common sense, will level the playing field to a great degree. Twelve to 15 years ago, you stood in a crowd and you saw these guys come in with their sheets and you would ask "Does he have an advantage over me?" or "Is he tied to a system?" or "Is he being hamstrung?" or "Is he being constrained?"

Today, you have electronic pricing in the crowds and it's not so confining, it's more of an advantage. And the guys who don't have this pricing at times lean on those other traders who do. But, when you're upstairs now, everybody can have that.

Q: Tony, along those lines, let's talk about the importance of software. Maybe you could talk about your commitment to developing state-of-the-art options trading software?

Tony: I developed my first software program in 1986. And then when I started my initial upstairs trading operation in 1988, I created additional software. That software was among the first for analyzing options on the screen and showing spread relationships. That software was taken and brought into a public product that's very popular today by some traders.

We have a long history of being involved in software. I built TradeStar, and that has gone through several generations of development.

Q: Tony, talk about your newest software and what benefits it will provide to electronic options traders?

Tony: Right now we are building a product, tentatively called Merlin, which will be on the market before 2000. It's a suite application, not unlike a product like Tradecast that is used for trading securities electronically.

It has windows for order entry, trade blotter, and your portfolio, but we also have market windows where you can have real-time live analysis of individual options. Lights flash on—we call them lamps—when there are edges. We also have alerts that you can program when certain profitable opportunities arise based on volatility or price. You just hit one button and it sends your order to the market.

Q: And this is available for the professional market maker, is that right?

Tony: Right. Currently, subsets of the suite—the quoting, the volatility management, the quote request responding module are. The quote request responder—is a whole avenue of software that level 2 traders would never get into. Because what it says is "Hey, there are brokers that need quotes in these options, you guys are responsible for providing them, so give them some." And the top-level guys will have to do that and the mid-level guys won't. They're doing it for the third-level guys who are looking for those quotes. Our software performs the task automatically for them.

Q: Tony, can someone who trades online today, someone who trades E-Schwab or Wall Street Access, be able to get a system like this so that they can see this front end in terms of pricing, risk analysis, and spread relationships and still send their order along online?

Tony: Yes, absolutely. This provides a tremendous advantage to the online investor. Just as the professional market maker needs to evaluate a risk reward profile, the individual investor also needs to do the same thing to be profitable and safe.

Q: Without the obligation of having to make a market!

Tony: Yes. It's a benefit that the individual investor enjoys. Our software allows the trader or investor to do the "what ifs," if you will, to look at the risk reward or the payouts on a real-time basis and then execute online.

Q: And basically to establish where the edge is?

Tony: And establish where the edge is. However, the edge for a professional is defined differently than an edge for a middle level or an end user where their time frame may be different. Whereas a retail user may sense a move in an underlying product, they may be willing to give up what we would call the professional's edge—an eighth or a quarter of a point to get on board ASAP. The real edge is to understand the market you're trading or the underlying product. What the software allows the investor to do is to establish a clinical, risk-analyzed look at the market in order to have a better entry point.

Q: Tony, do you feel it is fair to say that the average investor is at a critical point in time right now. Just as a year or two ago there was a revolution in trading equities in terms of moving from the conventional way of trading to an electronic trading platform. It seems we're just at the threshold of a revolution occurring in options trading with tremendous potential.

Tony: Howard, what is critical to trading on a screen— whether it is underlying stocks, futures, or options—is your software. Your software needs to make it as easy and fluid as possible to know your market and execute swiftly.

Q: When you get right down to it, the key to being a successful trader once you have a point of entry is just to simplify it: be able to react automatically.

Tony: That's right. And with options there's a lot more to simplify. Rather than having to go through six distinct clicks to get your point of entry, you want to get it down to one! When three things or six things happen, it presents the opportunity for you to make the one-click decision.

Q: So, you can respond automatically and just get yourself into the market. Obviously, the same thing happens when you want to exit. You don't want to have to fuss around when you think you're wrong. You want to be able to get out.

Tony: Risk management is important for digital day traders of stocks, but for options it is different. With equities, you're pretty much going home flat (without a position) each day. But with options, trading being flat is a luxury that is not necessarily possible. So risk management is critical. Thus, your analytical tools are crucial. The bigger your positions and the broader your coverage of options classes and underlying the more your analytics have to be addressed. Software is essential. First you need to have the right platform, then you need to really understand all the principles of options trading that go back to basic theory and strategy. Given that, then your software must be flexible with a good solid clearing firm to back you up. All in all, right now I could not be more bullish on the opportunities at hand regarding electronically traded options.

7

INTERVIEW WITH JOE CORONA

Joe Corona is an independent trader who is a member of a proprietary options trading group. He has traded options as a market maker on several exchanges and currently trades options electronically, primarily Eurex.

Q: Joe, what first attracted you to trading?

Joe: Initially, I liked the idea of being involved in a business that had a low entry cost, a low entry barrier. Basically, all you had to do was raise enough capital to open an account and lease a membership and you could start trading.

Q: When did you start trading?
Joe: 1982.

Q: Was your background in finance?
Joe: No, not at all. I was an education major. I had some friends who were involved in trading and they convinced me it might be something interesting for me to try. I started in what I thought was a temporary job while I was interviewing for a teaching position. Eventually, of course, I stayed.

Q: Did you start trading on the floor?
Joe: Oh, no, I started in the traditional way. I was a runner, then a phone clerk, a clerk for a broker, and eventually I worked for a market maker until another trader ultimately backed me.

Q: What then attracted you to trading? Was it the fact that you had all the leverage so you could make a lot of money or was it the intellectual challenge?

Joe: I enjoy playing the game, trying to figure things out. You know, the mental chess match aspect; trying to put together all the different pieces and predict what's going to make the markets move.

Q: Why did you choose to trade options?

Joe: At the time I started, the options markets were very sloppy (inefficient). There weren't a lot of people using any sophisticated tools. The PC age hadn't arrived yet. Traders were still figuring out things by hand or in their heads.

Q: We're talking 1980?

Joe: Yes. And being on the floor gave us a pretty good advantage. There were a lot of arbitrage possibilities. A lot of high return plays that you could do because the markets were so inefficient. Half the stocks traded didn't even have puts. There were calls only. So if you could think fast and calculate well there were many opportunities.

Q: What was your experience as a market maker like?

Joe: I enjoyed it a lot. I'm very competitive by nature and I liked being in the pit. And because the options market was in its infancy there were a lot of opportunities. This was at the time when the options were still traded on the 7th floor of the Board of Trade building. The CBOE was still a relatively small place. I mean the bull market had not started. It wasn't until August of 1982 when the trading volume started to pick up. So I have enjoyed evolving as a trader as the markets have matured.

Q: Now you've moved from being a market maker on the floor of the exchange. Actually you have traded on several exchanges, is that correct?

Joe: Howard, an options trader lives and dies by volatility. After the initial up move in stocks, the market went into a period of consolidation with low volatility. So I was attracted to the bonds that in the mid-80s were highly volatile. Interest rates were relatively high and it was an active trade. I went over to the bonds and traded bond options at the Chicago Board of Trade.

I've sort of always followed the volatility. With stocks, things became extremely volatile and then there was the crash. After 1987 there was a very dead period in the stocks and later in the bond options too. So I left and traded grain options in '88 and '89. It was a drought period, and consequently was extremely volatile. When that market died off, I traded options on currencies for a couple of years.

I traded Swiss, yen, deutsche mark, and British pound. With options it doesn't really matter. As an options trader, you know, some of the markets have different idiosyncrasies and nuances but, generally, option trading is option trading! It's all based on volatility.

Q: And now you've moved from having this wide range and experience on the floor as a market maker in different products to being part of a proprietary trading group trading electronically upstairs, is that correct?
Joe: Yes.

Q: Joe, could you talk about what the transition was like from being a market maker on the floor to being an electronic trader?
Joe: I didn't go directly from being a market maker on the floor to trading electronically in front of a screen. There was a step in between. In the early '90s I saw a lot of potential for trading in the European bond market. There was a lot of volatility and, as I said earlier, volatility is what attracts me. I

moved to London in late '93 and worked for a bank, trading over-the-counter bond options.

I traded over-the-counter bond options and exchange-traded options on all the European fixed income products. At the time, floor trading was still dominating. Needless to say, we had a Eurex terminal, and I would trade through it. I found it to be more efficient and a more level playing field. With pit trading, as you know, it wasn't always a level playing field as far as trade allocation. A lot of trades have to do with geography. If you're standing next to the broker who has the majority of the order flow, you see the flow and you get the good trades. Usually you have to fight tooth and nail for those spots, and even though I'm big enough to do that, I didn't care for it. I would tend toward the middle of the pit and run around. Many times I would turn the market or make the bid or offer and the trades wouldn't necessarily go to me: they'd go to the person standing next to the broker! What I liked about the concept of electronic trading was that it was electronically matched, first in, first filled. If you turn the market, you get the trade! Nobody could take the trade away from you.

I also liked the idea that there was no potential for out trades. It was matched real time. You didn't have to worry about keypunching, you didn't have to worry about clerks or clerical errors, all the things that haunt a floor trader. Every floor trader knows you spend hours every day going through statements finding key punching errors and having them corrected. Clerks make mistakes. Cards get lost. You have out trades! All these things hit your bottom line hard, and none of these things exist on an electronic platform!

Q: Joe, what is your daily activity like in front of the screen. How do you set up in the morning, what are you looking for in the market?

Joe: On an electronic trading platform you're not confined to one particular pit or the set of information that you can get out of that pit, which is mainly the order flow. Upstairs in an office you have access to a lot of information. So I come in at one o'clock in the morning, which is eight o'clock Frankfurt time. I can see what the Japanese markets have done. I can check the interest rates. I check all the different bond markets: what the U.S. bond markets did on Project A (CBOT), what the JGBs have been doing, the gilts, the BTPs (Italian bonds), anything that can possibly affect my market. I go through the news and look for additional market data. I check the foreign exchange market and the commodity prices. I see what kinds of news reports are coming out today and then I can go through the technical analysis. So in front of me I've got four or five screens: one that'll have news, one that will have charts, one that will have other markets, two that have my markets. So the big advantage you have being off the floor is that you can have access to all this information that's not readily available to you while you're physically standing in a pit.

Q: You trade mainly fixed income, is that correct?

Joe: Yes. I trade the German ten year, five year, and two year products: the Bund, Bobl, and Schatz. I trade all of them on Eurex.

Q: Do you have a favorite option strategy?

Joe: Howard, I try to tailor what I'm doing to what my idea is for the underlying market. What I like to do as a proprietary trader is take a view of the market and do whatever suits my particular view. So I don't have a particular strategy. I'll buy options or I'll sell options, depending on what my particular bias is for the underlying market. As a market maker, I trade like every other market maker does and I try to pick up as much theoretical edge as I can and keep the risk as flat as possible. I just try and retain as much theoretical profit and turn it into real profit when I can.

Q: What do you think is the future of trading options online?

Joe: I think it's definitely going to be huge. You can already see it happening in the equities—E*TRADE, online trading, Nasdaq level 2—all these electronic trading platforms that are currently available to the retail stock customer. There's a bit more difficulty with options because of the complexity of strategy that is involved. They are difficult to pin down from an algorithmic standpoint. I mean, for stocks, you buy, you sell, that's it. You know, with options you can buy and sell, there's calls and puts, there are spreads, there are different complex strategies that people like to implement. So I think that the technology has to catch up a little bit with options but I think for the same reasons I put myself in the electronic arena, the opportunities will be tremendous.

Q: What are the specific tactical demands of an electronic options trader?

Joe: The biggest thing I've found is the discipline required. It is paramount.

Q: Psychological discipline?

Joe: Yes, psychological discipline. You don't get the physical feedback from trading electronically. In a pit you're waving your arms, you're yelling, you know you're making a trade. You know you're taking risk! Trading electronically can feel "riskless," all you have to do is tap the mouse and you're trading! Nobody is screaming at you, you're not getting the physical feedback.

Q: That's what Tony Saliba said. The hardest aspect for him was the same thing. He just kept buying or selling options because all he was doing was clicking the mouse and he wasn't getting any physical feedback that he was accustomed to as a floor trader.

Joe: There's a lot of big problems that can happen with that too because you can pile up a lot of risk in a hurry just by tapping your forefinger. You know, it's the biggest thing I've had to teach myself since I've been doing this. And I've been doing this for over five years now. When you're in the pit you have the opportunity to move in and out seamlessly. Upstairs you can't do that, you can't turn around and trade as quickly. You can't trade like you're used to in a pit, so you must widen your time horizons. You must learn how to discipline yourself to keep your hands off the mouse when you're in an area where there seems to be only a small advantage. It's hard to do!

Q: How do you use technical analysis as it relates to your options trading?

Joe: What I do is basically divide my trading into two different areas: proprietary trading, which is mostly directional, with a viewpoint bias, and market making, which is more geared to gaining market edge.

I use standard technical analysis, nothing fancy. It depends on what my time horizon is. I'll look at the markets and then I overlay them with some fundamental political analysis plus what the central banks are doing and put that into my overall point of view. And once I have a directional bias I decide which option strategy to use.

Q: What sort of technicals are you looking at?

Joe: Just some real easy stuff. As far as longer-term trades, I look at bar charts, candlestick charts, moving averages, trend lines, and market profiles.

Q: What kind of time frames are you using, 30 days?

Joe: Yes, but I will also blend several longer-term frames.

Q: Are you looking at support and resistance levels in the market?

Joe: Yes, but it's hard for me to pin it down; it's not a straight package. It's as much an art as it is science. I don't have a particular system where a computer just plugs in and executes. I have things I like to do, I have patterns I like to trade off. I can get a buy signal based on a moving average breakout, a chart point breakout, or a volatility breakout. I really keep track of historical volatility and implied volatility, and base my trades on that quite a bit.

Q: If you see a breakout in volatility you'll buy the volatility?

Joe: Yes, I'll buy the volatility and take advantage of the pricing because all the different strikes aren't priced exactly the same. They trade at different levels depending on what type of market it is and what the current conditions are. So then you find the strategy that's most advantageous to you to take advantage of the breakout. Sometimes you'll couple a volatility breakout with a directional breakout and you'll take advantage of that as well.

Q: Joe, could you briefly describe what you feel is required for successful options trading from a psychological point of view? You mentioned discipline earlier.

Joe: I think you have to have a longer-term horizon, especially if you're making a transition from pit trading to trading electronically. A floor trader is probably at a disadvantage relative to someone who's just entering the business for the first time trading electronically because he's got to unlearn so much of the trading behavior from the pit.

Q: Someone from the pit's at a disadvantage?

Joe: I think so. You know the markets and you know what's involved with the markets and you know what makes the market go up and down, but you've got to train yourself not to trade like you do in the pit. You can't constantly trade!

What gives you an advantage on the floor doesn't matter upstairs. You've got to create your advantage elsewhere through research, technical analysis, or whatever! So the hardest thing is to become very unemotional and disciplined. Just learn to stay out of the market because there's nothing meaningful going on. If you have your parameters drawn, you're going to enter and exit well. Unless the market is at one of your levels, you won't get involved. Market making, as I said, is different. You get whatever the paper (order flow) gives you.

Q: You get theoretical edges?

Joe: Yes, and you deal with that at the time. But I think electronic trading really offers tremendous opportunity.

Q: What words of advice would you offer to someone who's planning to become an electronic trader of options?

Joe: If you were coming from the floor I would say that you have to try and implement some sort of technical or mechanical strategy or some filter to help you figure out what it is that makes you want to buy or sell a market. Make it as mechanized as possible to keep you from overtrading.

Sitting in front of the screen, you naturally, as a human being, figure if you're at work you should be doing something, so you feel like you should be trading. The next thing you know you're in a trade for really no particular reason. So again, I think you need to mechanize your criteria to keep you out of the market when it's not to your advantage.

Q: And if you didn't have floor experience, if you're just someone who's a serious investor, what would your advice be?

Joe: I don't think they have as much of a problem. I think a serious investor trades like an investor and that's sort of how you have to trade electronically. You know, they have whatever it is that gives them their idea for an investment: whether it's fundamental or technical information. They wait until they get it before they trade.

Q: And the electronic platform, do you think that would be an advantage to them in terms of their investment?

Joe: Yes, for a couple of different reasons. First of all, it lowers your costs dramatically. It's secure and instantaneous and you're not at the behest of a broker. You don't have to call anybody, you don't have to talk to anybody, you're not paying 25 bucks a side. There are currently places that are charging $5 a side for options on futures! You put the order in yourself, you execute it yourself. You get the confirmation instantly. You take control of your own financial destiny. The down side of that could be there's no one there to help you out when you're doing something stupid. There's no safety net. But this is a big boy's game, and it's really incredible.

You plug in your laptop in Jackson Hole or Key West, in Greece, or wherever you want. You dial up a brokerage firm Web site and have access to all the electronic exchanges instantaneously. If you need to do something in the gilt or bund or trade Sweden or Australia or Globex . . .

Q: So I get the feeling, Joe, that you really feel like we're at an exciting turning point for options trading?

Joe: Yes, I'm very bullish on the options market, and that's why I'm so deeply involved in it. I enjoyed the pit, I loved being down there with the other traders and screaming and yelling and all that, but I really think this is where the future is, especially with the introduction of ISE (International Securities Exchange).

PART THREE

MARKET ANALYSIS AND OPTIONS TRADING

8

TECHNICAL CONSIDERATIONS: STRATEGIES FOR PROFITABLE TRADING

The use of options creates versatility and opportunity for the investor. Options provide a wide range of strategies that can be as conservative or as speculative as you would like. Some of the benefits to you in trading options are the following:

- Options offer protection from a decline in your investment.

- Options increase income from equity investments.

- Options allow for the adoption of a position for big market moves.

- Options provide for the benefit of capturing a market move without putting up the full value of the investment.

- Options offer a sound investment vehicle for creating limited risk strategies.

As discussed earlier, options like stocks or futures can be used to participate in market movements; however, with options you can fine-tune the leverage, predetermine the risk, and create positions that closely resemble your own perspective of market conditions and potential.

It is important to remember that options are rights—but not obligations—to buy or sell a stock or futures contract for a specified price on or before a specified date. A call is the right to buy the underlying investment (a stock or future contract) and a put is the right to sell the underlying investment. An investor who buys a put or call is an option "buyer." An investor who sells a put or call is the option "seller."

To review, options are standardized contracts that give the buyer the right but not the obligation to buy or sell an underlying investment for a fixed price, called the "strike price," up to a specified date, which is the "expiration." An equity option usually represents 100 shares of the underlying stock and a futures option normally represents 1 contract. All of the options contracts we speak about in this book are traded on U.S. securities exchanges or electronic exchanges. These include the Chicago Board Options Exchange (CBOE), the Philadelphia Stock Exchange (PSE), the American Stock Exchange (AMEX), the Chicago Board of Trade (CBOT), the Chicago Mercantile Exchange (CME), and the combined futures exchanges in New York, Eurex, and the OM in Europe.

The price an investor pays for an option is called its "premium." This also represents the total potential loss to the buyer of an option. The seller of an option, however, receives the premium from the buyer but assumes an unlimited market risk.

All options expire on a specific date, which is called the "expiration date." The most commonly traded options are called American-style options and they may be exercised anytime between the date of purchase and the expiration date. The other form of option, a European-style option, only can be exercised during a specified period of time just prior to expiration.

BASIC OPTION STRATEGIES

The versatility of options allows you to take advantage of any directional movement in a market, as well as take advantage of a stagnant market. Deciding on what options to buy or sell, what combinations to use, and how much risk to take is called option strategy.

The basic option strategies begin with the purchase or sale of individual options. This is options trading in its simplest form. These strategies are used when the trader feels the underlying market is or will be trending strongly. From there the trader moves on to simple spread trading strategies and then on to more complex strategies that include several combinations of options. These spread strategies can be used to take a market position that reflects how the trader views the underlying market and where he or she thinks the market would be at the time of the option's expiration.

Because options are a wasting asset, that is, they lose their value at a certain time, options traders are always concerned with the volatility of the underlying market. You could say that volatility is the measure of how fast the market is moving. Markets can be trading quietly over time, changing from low volatility to high volatility or vice versa. The options trader needs to be aware of the volatility of the underlying product, which will be reflected in the premium of the option. A highly volatile market will have higher premiums for each options strike and, conversely, a quiet market will have lower relative premiums.

The options trader can take advantage of the changing volatility of the underlying product as well as the wasting effect of time on the option. These strategies, along with bull market and bear market strategies, are listed and illustrated below.

The graphs in Figures 8.1 to 8.35 are typical for options analysis. The horizontal axis represents the price of the underlying instrument and the vertical axis represents the profit or loss from the position.

Bullish Market Strategies

- *Long underlying.* This is an outright purchase of the underlying instrument. The profit and loss of this position is unlimited. For purposes of valuation, a zero probability of the underlying product is not considered. See Figure 8.1.

- *Synthetic long.* Buy a call and sell a put of the same strike price. Your profit increases as the market rises and is based on the difference between the exit price and the entry price. The loss increases as the market falls and is based on the difference between the exit price and the entry price. See Figure 8.2.

- *Buy call.* Buying a call at a strike price closest to the market price is called buying an at-the-money call. Buying a call with a strike price above the market is called buying an out-of-the-money call. Buying a call with a strike price below the current market is called buying an in-the-money call. Each of these calls provides unlimited profit potential and limited risk. See Figures 8.3–8.5.

- *Sell put.* Selling a put provides a limited profit potential and an unlimited risk. See Figures 8.6–8.8.

- *Bull spread.* Buy a lower strike call and sell a higher strike call or buy a lower strike put and sell a higher strike put. Both the profit and loss is limited. See Figures 8.9 and 8.10.

FIGURE 8.1 Long Underlying

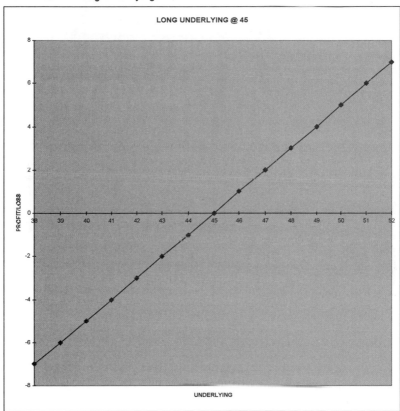

Days to Expiration: 64
Interest Rate: 7.15%
Volatility: 35%
Dividend: None

FIGURE 8.2 Synthetic Long

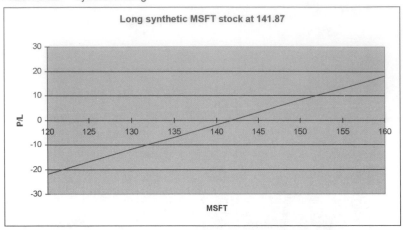

Long MSFT Aug 135 Call at **9.25**
Short MSFT 135 Put at **1.88**
Banking = **.50**
Synthetically Long Underlying at **141.87**
(9.25 – 1.88 - .50 + 135)

FIGURE 8.3   Buy Call

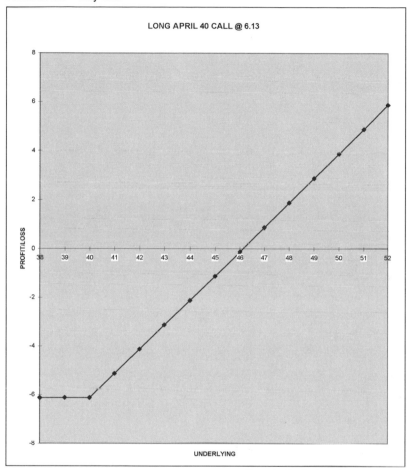

LONG APRIL 40 CALL @ 6.13

Days to Expiration: 64
Interest Rate: 7.15%
Volatility: 35%
Dividend: None

FIGURE 8.4   Buy Call

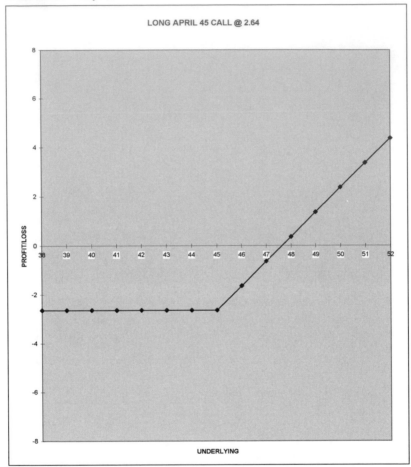

Days to Expiration: 64
Interest Rate: 7.15%
Volatility: 35%
Dividend: None

FIGURE 8.5   Buy Call

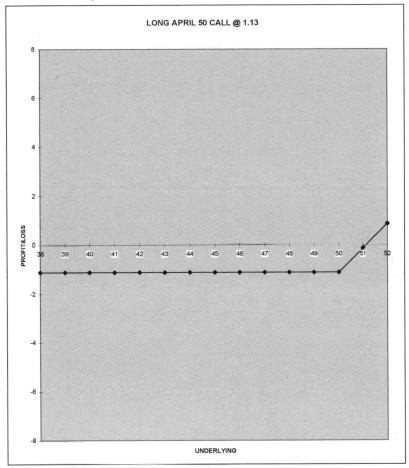

Days to Expiration: 64
Interest Rate: 7.15%
Volatility: 35%
Dividend: None

FIGURE 8.6   Sell Put

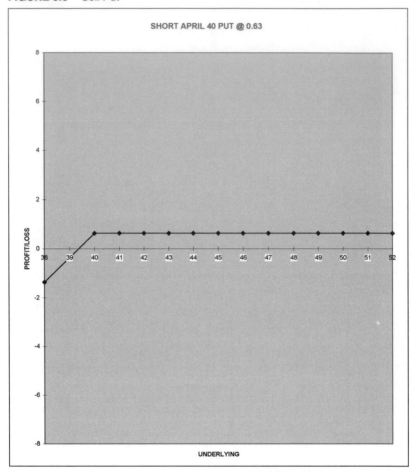

Days to Expiration: 64
Interest Rate: 7.15%
Volatility: 35%
Dividend: None

FIGURE 8.7   Sell Put

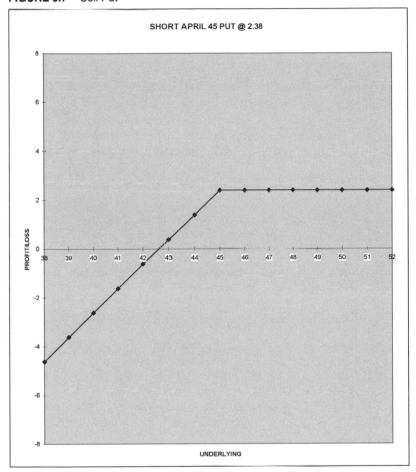

Days to Expiration: 64
Interest Rate: 7.15%
Volatility: 35%
Dividend: None

FIGURE 8.8   Sell Put

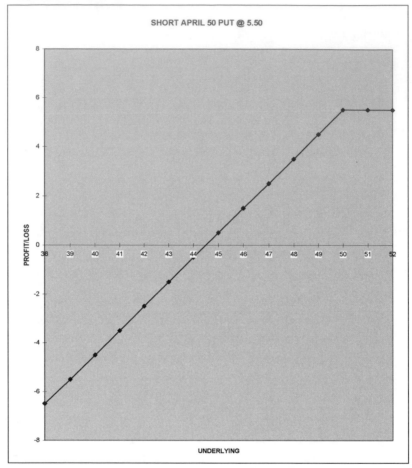

SHORT APRIL 50 PUT @ 5.50

Days to Expiration: 64
Interest Rate: 7.15%
Volatility: 35%
Dividend: None

FIGURE 8.9   Bull Spread Using Calls

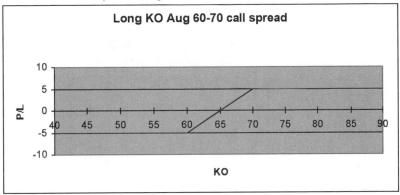

Long KO August 60/70 Call Spread
Long the Aug 60 Call at **10.13** and Short the
Aug 70 Call at **5.13**

FIGURE 8.10   Bull Spread Using Puts

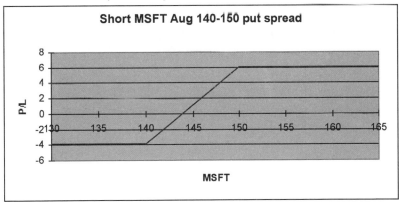

Short MSFT Aug 140/150 Put Spread
Long the Aug 140 Put at **3.50** and Short
the Aug 150 Put at **9.63**

Bearish Market Strategies

- *Short underlying.* This is an outright sale of the underlying product. The profit and loss is unlimited. See Figure 8.11.

- *Synthetic short.* Buy a put and sell a call with the same strike price. The profit increases as the market falls and is based on the difference between the entry price and the exit price. A loss increases as the market rises. The loss is based on the difference between the entry price and the exit price. See Figure 8.12.

- *Buying puts.* Profit increases as the market falls. The loss is limited to the amount paid for the option. See Figures 8.13–8.15.

- *Selling calls.* Profit increases as the market falls. The loss is unlimited and the profit is limited. See Figures 8.16–8 18.

- *Bear spread.* Sell a lower strike call and buy a higher strike call. You can sell a lower strike put and buy a higher strike put as well. The profit is limited and the risk is limited. See Figures 8.19 and 8.20.

Large Market Moves

- *Long straddle.* Buy a call and buy a put at the same strike price. This strategy will profit from a large move in either direction. The loss is limited to the cost of the straddle. See Figure 8.21.

- *Long strangle.* Buy a call and buy a put of a different strike price. The profit characteristics are the same as the straddle, however, if the market stagnates, you lose less than with a straddle. See Figure 8.22.

FIGURE 8.11   Short Underlying

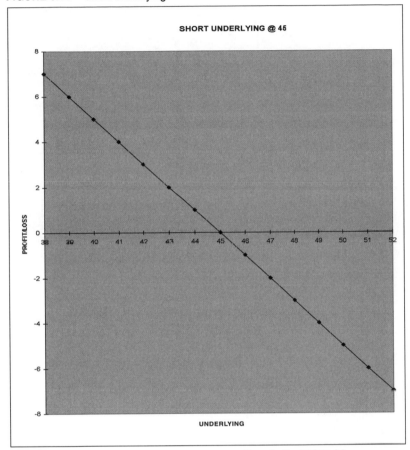

Days to Expiration: 64
Interest Rate: 7.15%
Volatility: 35%
Dividend: None

FIGURE 8.12   Synthetic Short

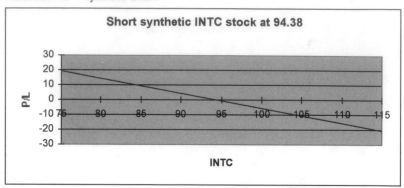

Short INTC Oct 90 Call at **6.50**
Long INTC Oct 90 Put at **1.87**
Banking = **.25**
Synthetically Short INTC Stock at **94.38**
(90 + 6.50 − 1.87 - .25)

FIGURE 8.13   Buy Put

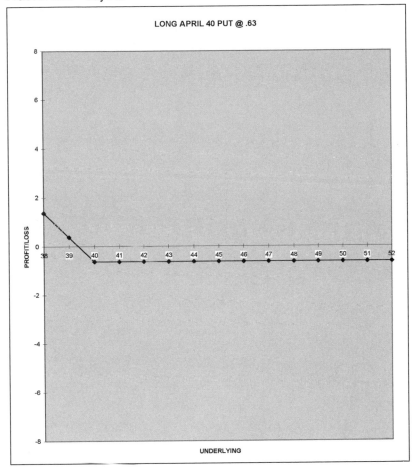

Days to Expiration: 64
Interest Rate: 7.15%
Volatility: 35%
Dividend: None

FIGURE 8.14   Buy Put

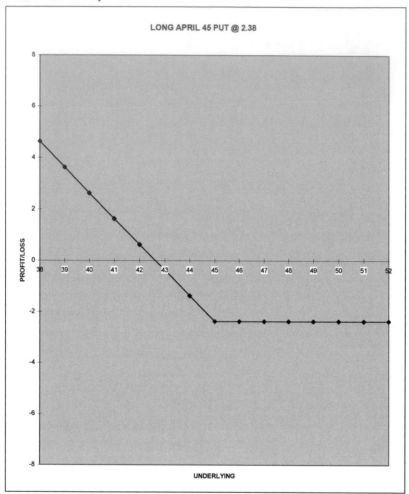

Days to Expiration: 64
Interest Rate: 7.15%
Volatility: 35%
Dividend: None

FIGURE 8.15   Buy Put

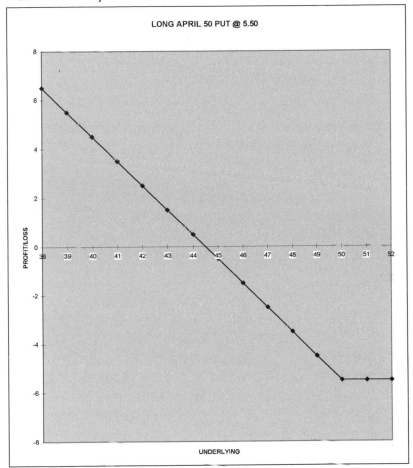

Days to Expiration: 64
Interest Rate: 7.15%
Volatility: 35%
Dividend: None

FIGURE 8.16   Sell Call

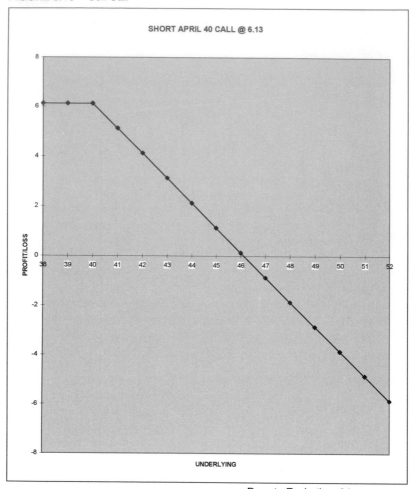

Days to Expiration: 64
Interest Rate: 7.15%
Volatility: 35%
Dividend: None

FIGURE 8.17   Sell Call

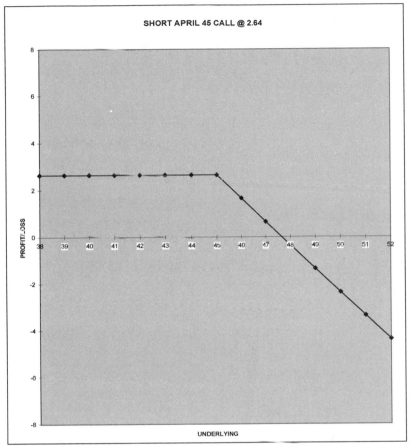

Days to Expiration: 64
Interest Rate: 7.15%
Volatility: 35%
Dividend: None

FIGURE 8.18   Sell Call

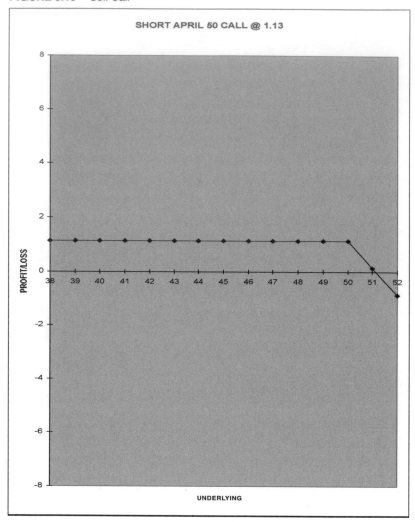

Days to Expiration: 64
Interest Rate: 7.15%
Volatility: 35%
Dividend: None

FIGURE 8.19   Bear Spread Using Calls

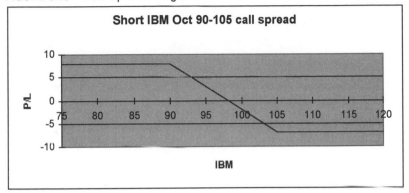

Short IBM Oct 90/105 Call Spread
Short the Oct 90 Call at **10.12** and
Long the Oct 105 Call at **2.12**

FIGURE 8.20   Bear Spread Using Puts

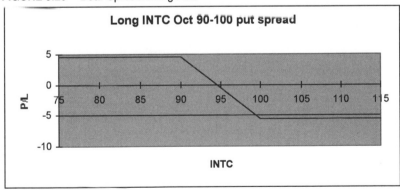

Long INTC Oct 90/100 Put Spread
Long the Oct 100 Put at **7.12** and
Short the Oct 90 Put at **1.62**

FIGURE 8.21   Long Straddle

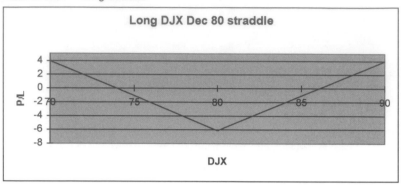

Long 1 DJX (Dow Jones) Dec 80 Call at **3.625**
Long 1 DJX Dec 80 Put at **2.5**
= Long DJX Dec 80 Straddle at **6.125**

FIGURE 8.22   Long Strangle

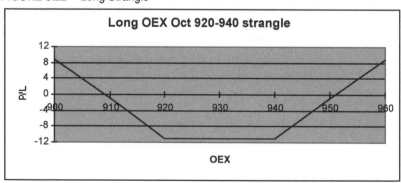

Long 1 OEX (S&P 100) Oct 920 Put at **5.125**
Long 1 OEX Oct 940 Call at **5.875**
= Long OEX Oct 920/940 Strangle at **11.00**

Volatility Strategies (Quiet or Sideways Markets or Changing Volatility)

- *Long butterfly.* Buying a lower strike call, selling two higher strike calls, and buying one even higher strike call. You also can buy a lower strike put, sell two higher strike put, and buy one even higher strike put. Maximum profit occurs if the market is near the middle strike price. This profit usually develops close to expiration. Maximum loss is cost of spread. See Figures 8.23 and 8.24.

- *Short straddle.* Sell a call and sell a put with same strike price. The profit is maximized if the market is at or near the strike price at expiration. The loss is open ended in either market direction. See Figure 8.25.

- *Short strangle.* Sell a lower strike put and sell a higher strike call or sell a lower strike call and sell a higher strike put. The maximum profit is realized if the market is between the strike prices at expiration. The loss potential is unlimited. See Figure 8.26.

- *Ratio call spread.* Buy a lower strike call and sell two or more higher strike calls. The maximum profit is realized if the market is at the higher strike price at expiration. The loss is proportional to the number of excess shorts in the position. See Figure 8.27.

- *Ratio put spread.* Buy a put and sell two or more lower strike puts. The maximum profit is realized if the market is at the lower strike price at expiration. The loss is limited on the upside but open-ended if the market falls. See Figure 8.28.

FIGURE 8.23   Long Call Butterfly

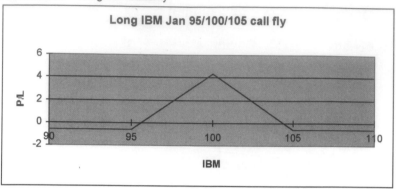

Long 1 IBM Jan 95 Call at **10.75**
Short 2 IBM Jan 100 Calls at **8.125**
Long 1 IBM Jan 105 Call at **6.125**
= Long IBM Jan 95/100/105 Call Butterfly at **.625**

FIGURE 8.24   Long Put Butterfly

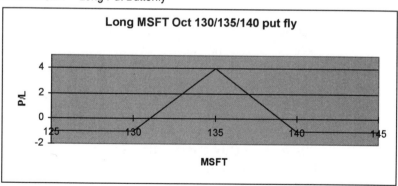

Long 1 MSFT Oct 130 Put at **2.5**
Short 2 MSFT Oct 135 Puts at **4.75**
Long 1 MSFT Oct 140 Put at **8.00**
= Long MSFT Oct 130/135/140 Put Butterfly at **1.00**

FIGURE 8.25   Short Straddle

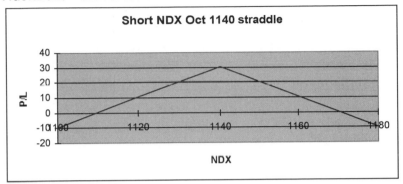

Short 1 NDX (Nasdaq 100) Oct 1140 Call at **15.00**
Short 1 NDX Oct 1140 Put at **15.50**
= Short NDX Oct 1140 Straddle at **30.50**

FIGURE 8.26   Short Strangle

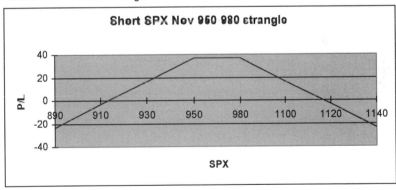

Short 1 SPX (S&P 500) Nov 950 Put at **16.625**
Short 1 SPX Nov 980 Call at **20.00**
= Short SPX Nov 950/980 Strangle at **36.625**

FIGURE 8.27   Ratio Call Spread

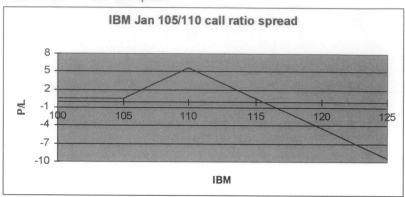

Short 2 IBM Jan 110 Calls at **2.00**
Long 1 IBM Jan 105 Call at **3.38**
= IBM Jan 105/110 Call Ratio Spread at **.62 (credit)**

FIGURE 8.28   Ratio Put Spread

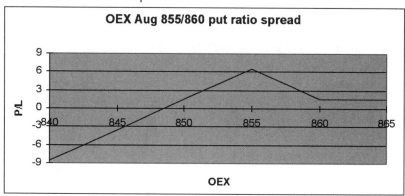

Short 2 OEX Aug 855 Puts at **1.75**
Long 1 OEX Aug 860 Put at **2.00**
= OEX Aug 855/860 Put Ratio Spread at **1.50 (credit)**

- *Call ratio backspread.* Short a call and buy two or more higher strike calls. This strategy is entered when the market shows signs of increasing activity with a greater probability to the upside. See Figure 8.29.

- *Put ratio backspread.* Sell a put and buy two or more lower strike puts. This strategy is entered when the market shows signs of increasing activity, with a greater probability to the downside. See Figure 8.30.

Now that we have an understanding of the risk profile and appropriate applications of basic option strategies, let's turn to the use of specific techniques and tactics of technical analysis to identify situations where options strategies can be utilized. The use of technical analysis can serve both to identify areas of risk and opportunity for the options trader.

FIGURE 8.29   Call Ratio Backspread

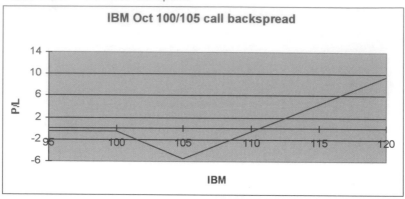

Long 2 IBM Oct 105 Calls at **2.13**
Short 1 IBM Oct 100 Call at **3.75**
= IBM Oct 100/105 Call Back Spread at **.50 (debit)**

FIGURE 8.30   Put Ratio Backspread

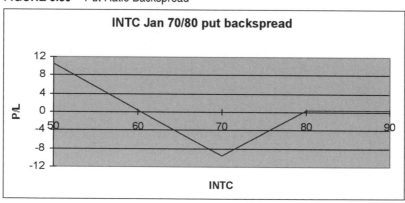

Long 2 INTC Jan 70 Puts at **1.00**
Short 1 INTC Jan 80 Put at **2.50**
= INTC Jan 70/80 Put Back Spread at **.50 (credit)**

9

CLASSICAL ANALYSIS AND OPTIONS

We have seen in the previous chapter that market bias, that is, reading a market as to direction, nondirection, or its volatility, is important to the options trader. The successful use of the strategies that we have previously discussed as well as the use of more highly sophisticated combinations requires that the trader make specific market judgments. I believe one of the most efficient methods to accomplish this is through the use of classical chart analysis.

Reading the underlying market correctly will make the appropriate options strategy a powerful tool for gaining profits and managing risk. I must caution the reader that my focus here is not on an in-depth study of all the technical aspects of markets, but rather it is on how chart analysis directly relates to the selection and use of option strategies.

TREND IDENTIFICATION

In broad strokes, markets are doing one of a few things at any moment in time. A market can be trending up, down, or be range bound. It may be doing this in an orderly fashion or with a great amount of volatility. Capturing profit resides in either correctly identifying a market's current status or knowing when the current status will change. The primary methods of identifying market status or its trend are the following:

- Trendlines

- Moving average

- Channel breakout

Trendlines

Simple trendlines are usually drawn from low to low to establish an uptrend, or from high to high to establish a downtrend (see Figure 9.1). Variations of this are using closes instead of lows or averaging daily ranges and using those points as references.

Moving Average

The oldest and best-known method of establishing a trend is the moving average (see Figure 9.2). Simply stated, a moving average is usually obtained by adding up a series of closes and dividing the sum by the number of days used in the series. The result tends to smooth the series of numbers and is an effective method of trend identification. Many variations are possible, such as changing the number of days in the series or using highs and lows in place of the closing price. The most popular approach is in identifying a trend when the close (or other variable) is over or under the average, thereby signaling direction.

FIGURE 9.1 Trendline

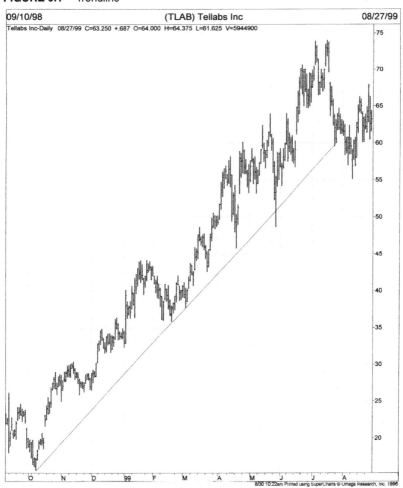

Channel Breakout

The channel breakout method can be used on its own or in conjunction with the other methods (see Figure 9.3). I define a channel as a series of days or weeks that is contained within an area of highs and lows. When a market moves through an area that has been established over a period of time, it signals a trend.

FIGURE 9.2 Moving Average

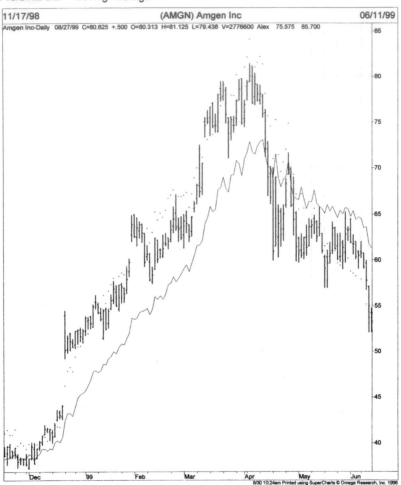

| 11/17/98 | (AMGN) Amgen Inc | 06/11/99 |

Amgen Inc-Daily 08/27/99 C=80.625 +.500 O=80.313 H=81.125 L=79.438 V=2776600 Alex 75.575 85.700

8/30 10:24am Printed using SuperCharts © Omega Research, Inc. 1996

Using the Trend

After we have drawn a trendline or created a moving average, there are a number of opportunities to use them. The obvious is to use the strategies that are clearly in tune with the
direction of the market. Another method is to focus on the mar-

FIGURE 9.3   Channel Breakout

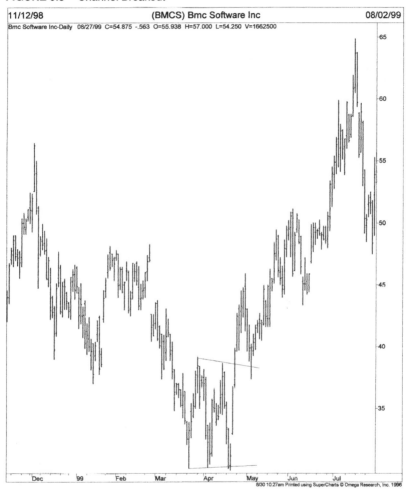

ket as it breaks or rallies to the trendline and use a directional options strategy as an entry point. Some traders will focus on the market breaking the trendline, signaling a change in trend. This is one way to enter such a market early. The moving average is treated in much the same way.

A nontrending market also offers opportunity to the options trader to use those strategies designed for sideways markets (see Figure 9.4). The options trader also must determine whether the market swings are volatile or not. Channel breakouts from this sideways pattern also offer an opportunity for early entry into a trending market.

A discussion about trends is important. All the top traders we have spoken to know or believe they know where the markets are relative to the trend. For example, the market is bottoming, topping, retracing, etc.

Each major up or down trend has three phases. They are:

1. Accumulation

2. Main phase

3. Distribution

Accumulation

Low prices, light volume, and small daily ranges characterize the accumulation phase of a market. The volatility is also to the low end of its historical range. This is a period when everything seems negative or uninteresting. This is a good time to consider the purchase of options and those strategies that would take advantage of increasing volatility (see Figure 9.5).

Main Phase

The main phase begins with a breakout and a sustained rally above the bottom area. Volatility and daily ranges expand and the market becomes quite active. Options traders can use those strategies that take advantage of increasing volatility and a trending market.

FIGURE 9.4 Sideways Channel

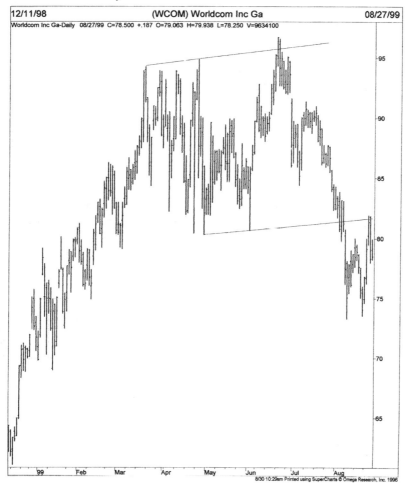

12/11/98   (WCOM) Worldcom Inc Ga   08/27/99

Worldcom Inc Ga-Daily 08/27/99 C=78.500 +.187 O=79.063 H=79.938 L=78.250 V=9634100

8/30 10:29am Printed using SuperCharts © Omega Research, Inc. 1996

Distribution

The distribution phase is characterized by large swings in the market, high volume, and high volatility. It's the beginning of a reversal of the market. Options traders should be looking at the high volatility and the probability of change in direction of the market (see Figure 9.6).

FIGURE 9.5   Accumulation Phase

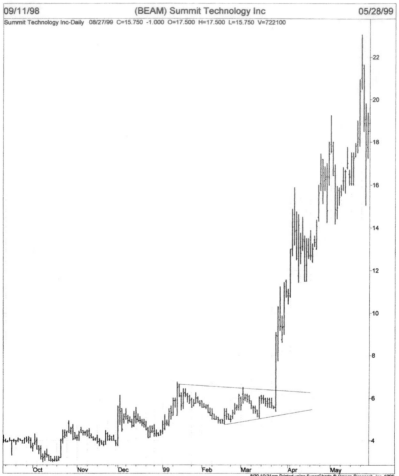

Support and Resistance

The channel pattern described above is a good example of support and resistance. It's easy to see the dynamics of the market as it repeatedly holds the lows and highs over an extended period of time. As the market breaks out of the channel, in this

FIGURE 9.6   Distribution Phase

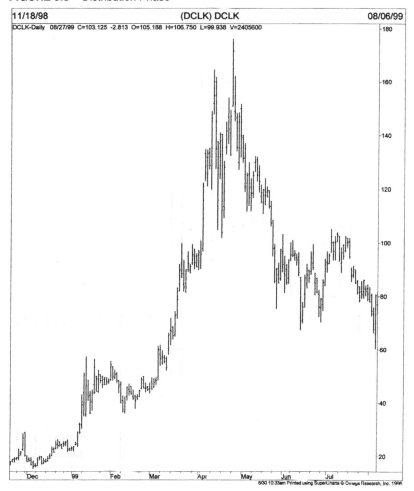

instance on the upside, aggressive buying and shortcovering drives the market to a point that attracts sellers and profit taking longs. The market begins a retracement toward the area of the top of the channel. Former buyers or potential buyers who saw the market move through the channel highs and missed the opportunity, begin to buy again near those highs. Similarly, a breakdown below the channel lows and subsequent rally forms resistance. Each of these occurrences is an opportunity to enter option strategies in the direction of the trend (see Figure 9.7).

Retracements

For many traders, one of the more difficult aspects of trading is developing the confidence to buy a breaking market or sell a market rally. We have seen earlier that support and resistance areas offer some benchmarks or reference points. There is, however, another trading method to take advantage of the market's normal retracements. Markets tend to retrace a third, a half, or two-thirds of the previous move (see Figure 9.8). Many traders get caught up in exact numbers (e.g., .382, .684, etc.) and forget that a few ticks is not meaningful in a dynamic and fluid marketplace. Options traders need only look for a general area in the underlying market to take advantage of a retracement. If a market retraces 50 percent of a previous move and shows signs of finding support, then the trader has a lot of information with which to make a high-percentage, low-risk options trade.

Reversal Patterns

The chart patterns that are created by traders during accumulation and distribution are called reversal patterns (see Figures 9.9 and 9.10). These patterns are seen time and time again. Rounded bottoms, tops, V or spike bottoms and tops, double or triple bottoms or tops, and head and shoulders bottoms and tops are the most common reversal chart patterns. Tops, on the other hand, are more often than not volatile, quick to form, and accompanied by lots of noise and attention (see Figure 9.11). If the options trader is aware of the development of these patterns, he or she can determine optimum option strategies to take advantage of these market conditions.

Support and Resistance

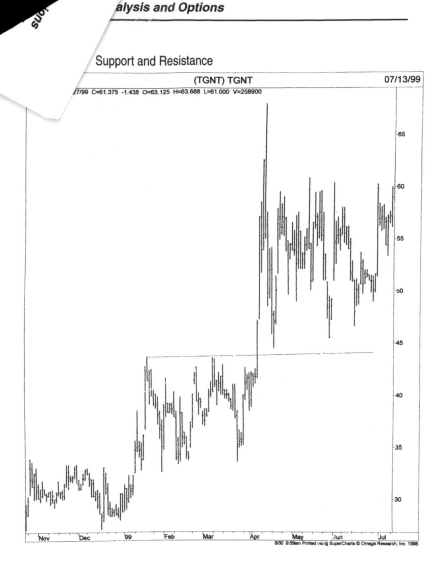

8/30 9:59am Printed using SuperCharts © Omega Research, Inc. 1996

Continuation Patterns

Continuation patterns generally present themselves throughout a trend. Their names are indicative of their shapes: triangles, flags, and rectangles (see Figure 9.12). After a significant market move in one direction, the market tends to pause as new sellers, attracted by the runup and short-term longs responding to their

FIGURE 9.8 Retracements

02/18/99	(QCOM) Qualcomm Inc	07/16/99

Qualcomm Inc-Daily 08/27/99 C=183.750 -7.000 O=193.000 H=195.875 L=183.375 V=3926700

8/30 10:36am Printed using SuperCharts © Omega Research, Inc. 1996

profits, begin to sell. This sell-off finds support and begins its climb to the high of this move, but falls short as more sellers are attracted. This tug-of-war over a few days or weeks begins to form one of the basic patterns. The options trader can take advantage of this phase in the market with several options strategies already discussed. Volatility plays or directional entries into the trend at good prices are possible at this stage.

FIGURE 9.9   Double Bottom

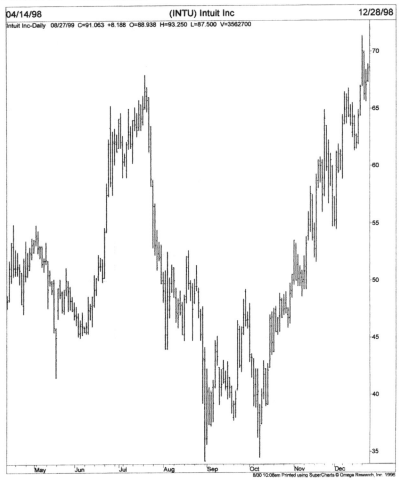

Successful options trading has more to do with knowing how to adapt to market conditions and strategy selection than possessing any particular trading system. These general principles of chart analysis have stood the test of time and continue to be used to form market opinion, and thereby create profitable option strategies.

FIGURE 9.10   Bottom Pattern

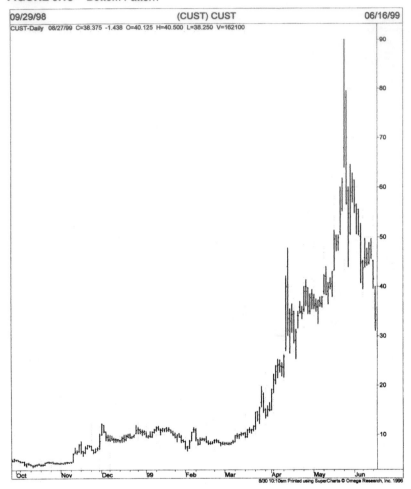

FIGURE 9.11   Double Top

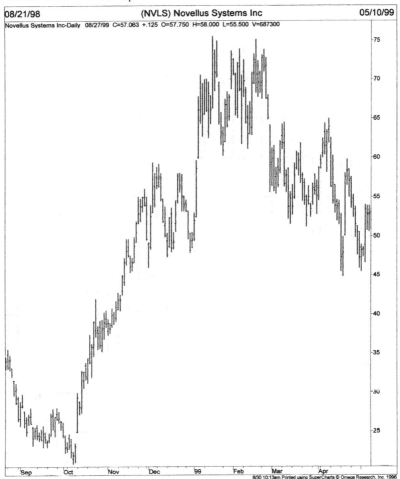

FIGURE 9.12   Continuation Patterns

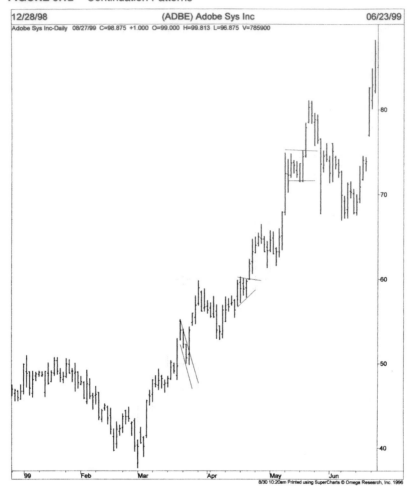

PART FOUR

PRINCIPLES OF PROFITABLE OPTIONS TRADING

10

THE PSYCHOLOGY OF SUCCESSFUL OPTIONS TRADING

It's my intention in this chapter to present what I believe you need to know, in the sense of having it burned into your hard drive to be a successful electronic options trader.

To begin, you must consider your options trading as a business, a serious endeavor that requires the same level of desire, commitment, and knowledge that any successful business project requires. Begin with writing a business plan.

THE BUSINESS PLAN

As with any business, content and substance—not wishful thinking—are called for. Write a business plan that contains the following:

- A clear statement of your business goals and philosophy

- A list of resources available now and in the future to pursue an options trading business

- Specific plans for the business—a description of your proprietary ideas, strategies, and tactics for advancing your goals

- A projected cash flow worksheet with a balance sheet that precisely presents your current financial position

- Identification of an ongoing mechanism for evaluation and future testing

ANALYTICAL SOFTWARE

The options trader needs to have the best possible analytical and execution software available. First Traders Analytical Solutions (FTAS) is, I believe, the best software soon to be widely available for execution. Omega Research produces a good analytical product.

TRAINING

To succeed in the highly competitive, high-energy arena of options trading requires a strong skill set and an ongoing commitment to be a continuous learner. As my partner, Bob Koppel, says, "Markets and traders keep on evolving; our job is to just keep evolving a little faster than everyone else."

There is no better place for serious options traders to get hands-on options training from knowledgeable market makers who have been directly involved in the setting up of trading rooms and electronic trading exchanges worldwide than at the

International Trading Institute (ITI) located in Chicago. ITI offers the highest level, state-of-the-art professional options training and consulting in the world. It has developed workshops in all key areas of options trading. A few of their intensive workshop offerings are:

- Reality of pit versus screen trading

- Profiles of screen-based trading environments

- Trading and pricing for the professional trader

- Options strategies for end users

- Screen-based trading strategies and techniques

Workshops are heavily content oriented and require student input—homework and passing a final exam that certifies screen-based trading proficiency. The training introduces participants to a screen-based trading environment, concentrating on familiarizing the student with viewing the market from an electronic perspective. Topics include:

- Hierarchy of participants

- Front-end risk management systems

- Execution of trades and orders

- Familiarity with all current electronic trading platforms

- Theoretical models

- Hedging and speculating with options

- Options strategies and relationships

The training is geared both to the novice and seasoned market professional. Programs range from day-long to 30 hours of focused, simulated electronic trading. Each student is immersed in a series of real-life training scenarios that builds electronic trading proficiency relating to risk management, inventory turnover, and overall profitability.

To learn more, contact ITI at www.itichicago.com.

SUCCESSFUL TRADING

In my long experience as a trader, market maker, and principle of my own team of proprietary traders I have found there are four essential requirements, from a psychological perspective, to be a successful trader:

1. Learn a proven trading methodology that is adaptable to a variety of market conditions.

2. Learn how to take a loss.

3. Learn the psychological skills of winning.

4. Learn the essential elements of a successful trading strategy.

Learn a Proven Trading Methodology That Is Adaptable to a Variety of Options Market Conditions

It is essential that each electronic options trader learn a trading approach or methodology that is personal, profitable, and consistent. Remember what Albert Einstein said: "Everything should be made as simple as possible, but not simpler." The purpose of keeping it simple is simple: so you can act!

Learn How to Take a Loss

Knowing how to take a loss automatically—without hesitation, fear, or second-guessing—is critical. For the trader, the essential issue that always needs to be resolved now is how to psychologically divorce him- or herself from the immediate and short-term trauma of incurring losses to pursue the long-term goal of profitability.

Traders need to overcome the following all-too-common self-defeating attitudes that often come into consciousness just at the moment of taking a loss:

- Holding yourself to an impossible standard

- Trying to please others

- Thinking in absolute terms—that is, total success or total failure

- Focusing on negative things

- Believing your childhood or past experience have programmed you for failure

- Demanding certainty of yourself and the market (there is no certainty ever, just high probability)

- Defining trading as impossible

- Representing a bad trade as a catastrophe

- Labeling yourself in a globally negative way rather than just looking at the trade.

Learn the Psychological Skill of Winning

The psychological skills necessary to become a successful options trader are listed below:

- Compelling personal motivation

- Goal setting

- Confidence

- Anxiety control

- Focus

- State-of-mind management

Compelling Motivation

Compelling motivation involves possessing the intensity to do whatever it takes to win at trading: to overcome a bad day or a temporary setback in the market in order to achieve your trading goals. It also means sticking to your trading plan and not allowing a momentary impulse based on fear or greed to control your decisions. Many options traders live on a roller coaster of inhibiting emotions. This is not the soil in which effective trading blooms.

Goal Setting

Goal setting is key for the trader. It focuses him or her on what is important in terms of motivation, outcome, and mechanics. Goals give direction and focus to the trading plan as well. You must know what you are trying to accomplish if you want to achieve an excellent trading result. You must be able to answer without qualification: "What am I trying to accomplish in the market; what is my strategy?" Goal setting allows you to make decisions without hesitation or ambiguity.

Ask yourself the following questions:

- Do I have in writing a clearly defined set of trading goals?

- Have I specifically done something to move me closer to achieving my goals?

- Do I have a clear idea of what I want to accomplish in the market?

- Do I concentrate on goals rather than procedures?

- Do I evaluate my progress based on accomplishment rather than activity?

As you think about your trading goals, remember that they should satisfy the following criteria for operational definitions of options trading goals:

- Specific—clear, precise, well-defined

- Time framed—stated within a specific time period

- Positive—stated in a way that is empowering

- Controlled—your goals should be completely within your control

- Realistic—it is not necessary to became the next George Soros . . . that was George's goal!

- Measurable—easily quantifiable

In my experience from training my own proprietary traders, I have found that when traders abandon their goals it is for one of the following reasons:

- Self-limiting beliefs

- Unresourceful state of mind

- Poor focus

- Ill-defined personal trading strategy

- Lack of physical and psychological energy

The answer to overcoming these trading obstacles always resides in psychological—rather than technical—analysis. But of course you already know this!

Confidence

When I speak of confidence I am not referring to cockiness, euphoria, or arrogance. Hubris in trading is lethal. Confidence, on the other hand, is essential and is the trader's natural expression of self-trust and being in control. It is effortlessly expecting a good result based on hard work, discipline, and an effective (tested and proven) methodology.

Anxiety Control

Sometimes I think anxiety was invented just for trading! There are so many anxieties the trader has to confront and master in order to be effective and apply a proven strategy.

Focus

Figure 10.1 reveals graphically the focus that is necessary for successful day trading results.

FIGURE 10.1   The Successful Options Trader's Focus

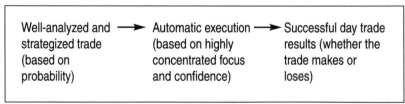

State-of-Mind Management

To be successful at day trading, you must constantly trade from a state of mind that allows you to maintain a high level of self-esteem, unshakable confidence, and laser-straight focus. This state of mind is characterized by being relaxed, focused, without anxiety, self-trusting, and resourceful. (See Figure 10.2).

FIGURE 10.2   The Successful Options Trader's State of Mind

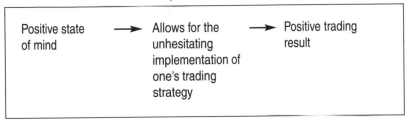

A positive state of mind is the result of consistently processing positive verbal attitudes, beliefs, and images that will enhance one's trading performance. To develop a positive state of mind:

- Expect the best of yourself.

- Establish a personal standard of excellence.

- Create an internal atmosphere for success based on visual, auditory, and feeling (kinesthetic) imagery that enhances performance.

- Communicate positively and effectively . . . with yourself! See yourself as positive, resourceful, and self-empowering.

- Rehearse a system of personal beliefs that can enhance your state immediately.

The psychological skills that are necessary to trade options successfully require ongoing commitment and conditioning. They must be practiced day in and day out. I have been keeping up-to-date charts by hand in more than 20 different markets for more than 25 years. Technical analysis is very important. It is not, however, in my opinion, as important as working through the psychological and attitudinal issues of trading in general and options trading in particular. (See Figure 10.3.)

FIGURE 10.3   The Syntax of Successful Options Trading

Well-Analyzed Trade

+

System of Empowering Personal Beliefs and Attitudes

+

Proper Execution Based on Positive Focus

+

Decisive, Resourceful State of Mind

+

Successful Trading Performance

LEARN THE ESSENTIAL ELEMENTS OF A SUCCESSFUL OPTIONS TRADING STRATEGY

As a profitable options trader it is important to be able to distinguish between trading strategy and trading tactics.

Strategy is the process of determining your major trading goals and then adopting a course of action whereby you allocate the resources necessary to achieve those ends. *Trading tactics* is the process of translating broad strategic goals into specific objectives that are relevant to a single component of your trading plan.

The essential elements of a successful options trading strategy are:

- Assumes personal responsibility for all market actions

- Takes into consideration your motivation for trading

- Allows you to trade to win

- Establishes a clear, precise plan of action

- Creates a point of focus

- Automatic, effortless in its implementation

- Manages risk and assumes losses

- Allows for patience

- Practical orientation—profit oriented

- Allows you to produce consistent results

Assumes Personal Responsibility for All Market Actions

Traders often say they "make a profit" but "take a loss." The reality, of course, is that we make both. You, the trader, produce the results. This fact may seem obvious. However, I can assure you, based on my 25 years of experience, having worked with hundreds of traders, it is the rare trader who truly lives by this credo! It isn't your broker, your brother-in-law, the board chair of the Fed, the fill, the computer, the unemployment report—it is you! It's a simple fact that must be understood in the adoption of any trading strategy: *You* are responsible for the results. Good or bad, the buck stops (and starts) here!

Takes into Consideration Your Motivation for Trading

It is essential that your options trading approach takes into consideration your motive and motivation for trading. In addition, it is imperative that your method feels "right," which is to say it is consistent and congruent with your personality. If it doesn't feel natural, it is like taking a ten-mile hike in boots that are two sizes too small. Ask yourself exactly why you want to option trade? Is your personality and approach suitable?

Establishes a Clear, Precise Plan of Action

The recipe for success in trading is a simple one. Your plan of action needs only three elements:

1. It identifies a signal (opportunity).

2. It allows you to take immediate action (buy or sell).

3. It allows you to feel good no matter what the result as long as the trade was consistent with your specific method or technical bias and was based on probability.

Most traders, however, experience hesitation or doubt just at the moment of action. The way to overcome this is to have a crystal clear point of focus, which allows you to resolve the omnipresent internal and external hindrances.

Creates a Point of Focus

Staying fixed on your particular approach, method, or system is what will allow you to resolve all the debilitating emotions you experience while option trading. It is exactly disciplining yourself to refocus back to your particular method, numbers, system, etc., which helps you resolve your natural feelings of anxiety as you are experiencing them. The essential point is you must know what you are looking for and what you are looking at in the market. You must be able to distinguish the signal from the noise, and high-probability trades from low-probability trades.

Automatic—Effortless in Its Implementation

The way all the hard work you have done as a trader pays off, in my opinion, is by being able to act absolutely, automatically, and effortlessly in the market when you have a high probability signal. The discipline is to hard wire your neurological system to act at just these times. By being in a position to "catch" those trades, you will find your need to tell colleagues about the great trades that got away has been neutralized!

Manages Risk and Assumes Losses

The one constant shared by all traders is that they take losses. You can't be afraid to lose. Truly, I love the market to take me out and hit my day trading stops. I challenge it to do no less. Do I like to lose? Hell, no! But if the market takes me out, I have paid for some very valuable information. Of course it goes without saying my losses are always circumscribed.

Allows for Patience

Following your signal religiously teaches you to have patience rather than getting caught up in the minute-to-minute emotions of trading. The key to success here is to give yourself the distance to make decisions that are based on thoughtful process, method, and strategy rather than on the exciting emotional gyrations of the market.

There are certain characteristics of a mindset that I believe are essential to creating success in the markets or creating consistency. To me, success as a trader is consistency. There is an often-used saying on the floor of the exchanges that "traders just rent their winnings." As you know, there are many traders who have reached the stage of development where they can put together a substantial string of winning trades for a day, weeks, or even months, only to lose all or most all of their hard-won equity in a few trades and then start the process all over again. If a trader hasn't neutralized his susceptibility to give his winnings back to the market, then he is not what I define as a successful trader.

—Mark Douglas, author, *The Disciplined Trader*

Practical Orientation—Profit Oriented

Many traders get bogged down in the theoretical accuracy of their particular systems. This is not necessarily important. What is important is performance. Making money supersedes attachment to a particular ideological or technical bias. I believe Winston Churchill said it best: "It is a socialist idea that making profits is a vice; I consider the real vice is making losses."

Allows You to Produce Consistent Results

Although in trading you can never really have certainty, paradoxically, in order to operate effectively, you must act with certainty, which is to say decisively at the point of decision. Consistency in trading derives from applying a proven method without fail every time a signal is generated. Your trading system provides the organization in order to allow you to identify and exploit opportunities, to achieve consistent results. It goes without saying, the rest is up to you! As Anthony Robbins has written in *Personal Power:*

> The difference between those who succeed and those who fail isn't what they have—It's what they choose to see and do with their resources and their experiences of life.

Accordingly, your trading strategy should allow you to open your eyes and see market opportunities . . . so that you can act!

Options Trading Is the Ultimate Chess Game

Trading options is a challenging activity based on brains, guts, and timing. Now ask yourself the all-important question:

Do you have what it takes? Leo Melamed has written (*Melamed on the Markets,* Wiley 1996):

> There is much to being a successful trader. There are many rules to be applied and many lessons to be learned. There must be a willingness and ability to learn, to comprehend fundamentals and statistics, to grasp technical applications, to develop an inner trading sense, to accept defeat and live with victory. But most of all, there must be present a multitude of inborn characteristics relating to the trader's personality, psychology, emotional equilibrium, courage, and patience.

> Ask yourself these questions:

- Are you a person who can easily make and live with your decisions?

- Do you thrive on intellectual challenge?

- Are you of an independent mind?

- Can you afford to take risk and not be intimidated by it?

If you feel you have what it takes to trade options, then trading electronically may be the right choice for you. There is an old trading adage that states "the market turns opinions into opportunities for those who have the courage to act."

Success in Trading.

TRADESTAR II OPTIONS SIMULATOR USER MANUAL

GETTING STARTED

Getting into TradeStar II

TradeStar II (T$II), is a Windows-based trading simulator. It is accessed like any other Windows operation, by double clicking the TradeStar II icon in the program manager. Once you activate the T$II icon, it prompts you to insert your disk and requires you to enter a password.

Trade$tar II Logon

Please enter your Name and Password.

(If you have just inserted a new disk, please choose your password by typing one now.)

Name: [   ]   [OK]

Password: [   ]   [Cancel]

This password is chosen by the user the first time the blank disk is used. Each time thereafter, this name and password is required to run the application with that disk. Next, the computer begins to configure the system. Once this is complete, the scenario screen appears, and this allows you to choose the desired scenario.

Choosing a Scenario

Once the scenario screen has appeared, the student then can access new and saved scenarios by choosing from the bottom function arrow. By clicking the arrow, the student may choose either "New Scenarios" or "Saved Scenarios." First choose from the "New Scenarios," the "Saved Scenarios" option is explained in the section on saving scenarios.

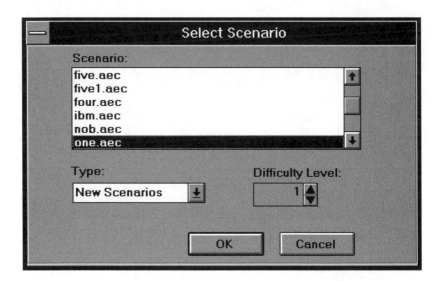

The student must then choose which scenario to use from the list in the upper right corner of the scenario screen. It is important to note that the student must not change the names on the left side of the scenario screen.

Choosing a Difficulty Level

Before clicking the "OK" button, the student must choose the difficulty level he or she wishes to use for the scenario. Note: Once a difficulty level has been chosen it cannot be changed for the remainder of the trading day. The student can choose a level between one and four by using the up and down arrows or by highlighting the number with the mouse and entering the desired level. Once the desired level has been chosen, as well as the correct scenario, the student may enter the trading simulator by clicking the "OK" button in the lower right-hand corner. This activates the simulator, and the student then begins a new trading day (unless a "Saved Scenario" is chosen, at which point that scenario would begin from the point where it has been stopped).

USING THE TRADESTAR II SCREENS

The Manual Execution Bar

Although most of the activity required by the student can be done with the mouse, many other activities require the student to use the manual execution bar. The manual execution bar is located at the bottom of the computer screen.

In itself, the bar is not a screen. Rather, it is a part of the desktop and cannot be resized or moved around. The manual execution bar has multiple functions. First, it acts as a way for the student to manually execute orders and to customize orders regarding price, quantity, and type of order. Second, the manual execution bar allows the student to manually make markets in options and option spreads.

Using the Manual Execution Bar for Execution of Trades

While using the simulator the student will use the mouse to activate cells in the market screen in order to make trades (this is discussed in more detail in the section called "The Trading Screen"). There are two ways a student can enter an order; either by clicking the option with the mouse and then using the manual execution bar, or by clicking one of three buttons on the bottom center of the manual execution bar. The button that allows the student to execute a trade is marked "E" for execution. When the execution button is clicked, the manual execution bar will set itself for execution of an order. The student must then click the desired option with the right mouse button. Two other buttons are located next to the execution button: "M" for make market and "X" for exercise options. These are discussed in greater detail later in this section. When the student clicks an option once, the manual execution bar displays on the left-hand side of the bar which option was chosen, its price, a default quantity of ten, and the choice to buy or to sell the chosen option.

The student must first choose whether to buy or to sell the chosen option. This is done by clicking the "buy" or "sell" buttons located at the far left. The option's price is shown in a white box with upward and downward arrows on the right-hand side of the box. These arrows allow the student to change the price of the option if he or she wishes to either make a different offer or to put an order in the order book at a different price (this is discussed in the section called "The Order Book"). The up arrow increases the price, and the down arrow decreases the price. Alternatively, prices may be entered by clicking the price box once and entering a price with the keyboard. A small gray box outlined in black-marked "Market" allows the student to buy or sell that option at the current market price. If there is an "X" in the box, it means that the student is buying or selling at the market price. In this case, the numbers in the price box will go gray and match the current market price. The quantity also appears in a similar white box with arrows that allow the student to adjust the quantity to buy or to sell. Finally, the student must decide what kind of order to use.

Three options are available including a fill or kill, "GTC" (good 'till cancel), or "IOC" (immediate or cancel). The student can choose between the different orders simply by clicking the arrow located above the expiration date. A drop down menu will appear, and the student can choose between the different orders simply by clicking the desired type. All "GTC" orders automatically go to the orderbook and remain there until filled or until the student deletes the order entirely. Once the orders are complete, the student then clicks the buy or sell button, and the order is sent. At the bottom of the manual execution bar, a message will appear that states that the order is sent. Note: The student uses this same process for the underlier and option spreads.

Making Markets Using the Manual Execution Bar

When the student wishes to make a market in an option or option spread, the student can use one of two different techniques. The student may either click the option or spread with the left mouse button, or click the button at the bottom of the manual execution bar marked "M" for make market and subsequently click the desired option or spread with the left mouse button. Either of these procedures will activate the market making segment of the manual execution bar.

The bar will display two white boxes with the upward and downward arrows. As described in the previous section, these arrows allow the student to adjust the prices for the markets that they make. Between the two boxes, another set of upward and downward arrows can be found that adjust the prices for both the bid and the ask. Above the white boxes, the student will find two gray outlined boxes: one marked "bid" and the other marked "ask." When both of the boxes have an "X" in them, the student may make a two-sided market. By clicking the boxes, the student can remove the "X" and make a one-sided market in either the bid or the ask. Once the student has completed the pricing of that market, he or she only needs to click the "make market" button to send prices into the market.

A student knows which market is his or hers by the color of its cells. Because each machine is set up with different color schemes, it is important for the student to consult with a labtech to verify the color scheme for that computer.

Exercising Options Using the Manual Execution Bar

When a student wishes to exercise an option, he or she can choose the option with either the right or left mouse button and then click the "X" button for Exercise. Once the student has chosen to exercise an option, the exercise option segment of the manual execution bar activates.

The student can choose the volume of options to exercise by using the aforementioned up and down arrows located on the right side of the white box. Once the student has chosen the appropriate volume, then he or she need only to click the exercise button and the execution will commence.

Other Uses of the Manual Execution Bar

A button marked "P", the Pause button, is located at the far left-hand corner at the bottom of the manual execution bar. To pause the scenario, the student can click the pause button and the scenario will stop at that point. It should be noted that each time the student clicks the pause button, the program records both the presence of a pause and the time elapsed during the pause.

At the bottom center of the manual execution screen is a clock. This simulator clock gives the time of the trading day within the simulator. Simulator time is approximately 20 actual minutes per simulation hour. The trading day begins at 9:00 AM simulation time, and ends at 5:00 PM simulation time. In real time, one trading day lasts approximately 2 hours and 40 minutes (without pausing).

The Trading Screen

The trading screen is separated into three different screens: the underlier market screen, the options market screen, and the spread market screen. These are not separate windows, but rather, they are contained in the trading screen and are separated by window splits that can be moved to increase or to decrease the size of the screens by using the mouse.

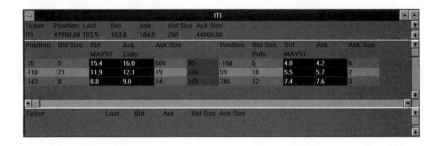

The underlier market is located at the top of the trading screen. It shows the current bid and ask for the underlying stock, the current bid and ask size, and the current price. Because this is an exercise in making markets in options, the student cannot make markets in the underlying. However, the student can make standing orders for the underlying, as discussed in the section "The Order Book Screen." In order for a student to buy or sell stock at the current price, he or she need only double click the bid or ask with the right mouse button, and the student will have bought or sold 1,000 shares of the underlying. 1,000 is the default amount offered when "double-click" buy or sell is used. If a different amount is desired, then the student must use the manual execution bar as discussed earlier. Note: If there are less than 1,000 shares available on either the bid or the offer, the "double-click" default will buy or sell whatever the quantity up to 1,000.

The options screen is broken up into cells much like a common spreadsheet. It is grouped by month and then by strikes in ascending order. Calls are found on the left side of the strikes, and puts on the right. For both calls and puts, the current bids and asks are listed and change as the market changes.

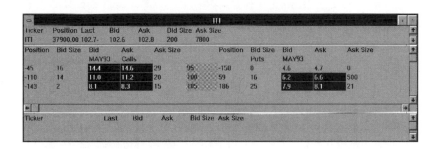

To buy or to sell at these prices, the student follows the same procedure for the options as for the underlying. By double clicking the right mouse, the student buys or sells ten calls or puts at the market price. Ten options is the default number. If the student wishes a different amount, he or she must use the manual execution bar. This can be done in one of two ways: After an option is chosen (by clicking it only once), its current market is displayed in the manual execution bar. To change it, the student can highlight those prices using the mouse and type in the new prices. Alternatively, the arrows on the right sides of the bid and ask box may be used to adjust the prices. The bid/ask size also can be determined using the same method. Once this is done, the student can click the "Make Market" button or push enter on the keyboard. The student can make a one-sided market by only changing the bid or ask (remove the "X" in the box) and then clicking the "Make Market" button (or "Enter").

There are many nuances to the options screen that the student can utilize to maximize efficiency while getting a better understanding of how options markets operate. A series of columns can be accessed that the student may want to utilize while trading. For example, if the student would like to use a theoretical value based on his or her own perception of volatility, the student can include that theoretical value and those volatility assumptions by first choosing where to put the column. For instance, if the student wishes to place the "own theoretical value" column between the put and call market prices, then he or she simply needs to double click the column heading of either the puts or calls and a pop-up screen will appear.

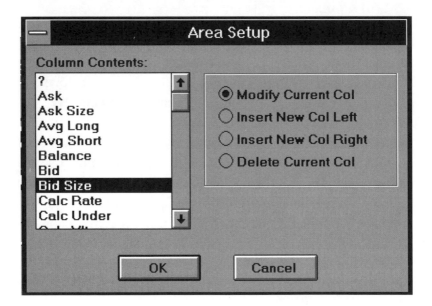

The pop-up screen contains a list of all the possible columns the student can include in their trading screen. It allows the student to insert the column to the left or right of the existing column. Furthermore, he or she may replace that column with a new column or delete that column entirely. Some of these columns provide information on the bid and ask size, real theoretical value, real volatility, implied volatility, etc. The student must remember that these are learning tools and, unless specified by the instructor, they should not be used while trading on the simulator.

The student is prompted to make markets during the simulation. The column marked "?" has an arrow that appears periodically in each option. It only appears for a short time, and the students response time is recorded on the trading log. Therefore, it is vital that the student pay close attention to this column.

The third segment in the trading screen is the options spread market screen, which is located below the options screen. The option spread screen gives the current markets in the option spreads. The scenarios in which students are trading are named corresponding to the spreads that are quoted here. For a more detailed description of the scenarios, it is important that the student consult with the instructor before beginning a new scenario. Using the option spread screen is much like the options and underlier screens with one exception, the student cannot make a market in an option spread unless he or she is requested to do so. When a market for a "90-100 Call Butterfly" is requested, the student may then make a market in that spread by using the manual execution bar in the same way that he or she made markets in the individual options. The student may also make one-sided markets if it is requested. For example, if the bid on the 90-100 butterfly was 2.5 and the ask is left blank, the student may quote the ask and vice versa. A student may change an existing market by using the manual execution bar, using the same method as described before, to make a new market in that options spread.

The Jet Screen

The Jet screen is the underlier market ticker. Prices and quantities traded pass across the screen as the transactions occur.

Jet				
ITI 1100	ITI 1100×81	ITI 3500		ITI 15500
101.5	101.5	101.6		101.6

The student must remember that Trade$tar II is a simulated market with other market participants. These "simulated" traders' activities are recorded and make up a significant part of the market. The jet shows neither whether those contracts were bought or sold nor to whom. It is up to the student to analyze prices and quantities and determine their effects on the market. The jet screen is a separate window, and its size can be adjusted like any other window by using the mouse and the cursor to push and pull the window's extremities. As the screen may begin to become cluttered with different windows, the student may decide to conserve space and eliminate the jet screen altogether by double clicking the upper left hand corner.

The Cascade Screen

The cascade screen works in a similar fashion to the jet screen, and it also is a market ticker. However, it records all transactions that occur in the scenario between the student and the other market participants.

```
┌──────────────────────────────────────────────────────┬───┬───┐
│  ─                         Cascade                     │ ▼ │ ▲ │
├────────────────────────────────────────────────────────┴───┴───┤
│ 12:07   ITI    101.6  15500                                   ↑ │
│ 12:10   ITI    101.6  10900                                     │
│ 12:10   ITI    101.6  2600                                      │
│ 12:10   ITI    101.6  5400                                      │
│ 12:12   ITI May 105 C  7.5  7  Bought from VINCE                │
│ 12:12   ITI May 100 C  10.4  10  Bought from VINCE              │
│ 12:12   ITI May 100 C  10.4  6  Bought from VINCE               │
│ 12:12   ITI May 105 C  7.3  5  Sold to VINCE                    │
│ 12:13   ITI    101.6  4800                                      │
│ 12:14   ITI    101.4  1000  Sold to BOB                         │
│ 12:15   ITI May 100 C  10.4  18                                 │
│ 12:15   ITI May 105 C  7.8  24                                  │
│ 12:15   ITI May 95 P  4.6  10  Sold to VINCE                    │
│ 12:15   ITI    101.4  1000  Sold to BOB                         │
│ 12:16   ITI    101.6  10500                                     │
│ 12:16   III May 100 C  10.4  4                                  │
│ 12:17   ITI May 100 P  6.5  8  Bought from VINCE              ↓ │
└─────────────────────────────────────────────────────────────────┘
```

Information provided by the cascade include: price, contract (both options and underlying), number of contracts traded, and with whom the contract was transacted. The student may find that this is a better way of keeping track of transactions. These transactions are recorded and the student has the ability to scroll up and down the cascade to review the activity. In fact, it is an excellent way for the student to keep track of what he or she bought or sold and at what price. Again this is a tool, one of many that the student will find quite useful while operating the simulator. The student may want to forgo the use of the cascade to increase his or her own difficulty and practice trading without such a luxury. Like the jet, the cascade window can be sized to the student's convenience by using the mouse. If the student does not wish to use the cascade window, it can be closed like any other window in the simulator.

The Order Book

The order book is a screen that records resting or standing orders that the student has entered using the manual execution bar.

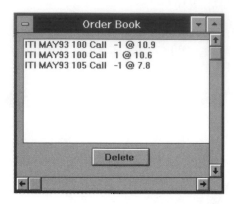

All orders that are GTC are automatically placed in the order book and remain there until they are either filled completely or deleted by the student. To delete an order the student simply must highlight the specific order and click the "Delete" button, which is located at the bottom of the order book window. To change an order, the student must delete that order and reenter the order with the desired changes. If the student does not delete the erroneous order, it remains in the order book and is filled when the market reaches that order. Orders may not be filled completely. The student may find that an order to buy 1,500 shares of the underlying will only be partially filled. In this case, the remainder of the order stays in the order book until another market participant hits that market. The orders are organized in ascending order. First the strike, then the calls and puts, and last is buy or sell. The underlying has the buy orders first and then the sell orders. Unlike all the other screens, the order book's size cannot be altered, but it can be minimized. As in every other Windows application, the windows can be moved around the screen to maximize the space available on the screen.

The Summary Statistics Screen

The summary statistics screen, or statistics screen, records and tracks the overall risk profile of the position that the student has acquired at that time, as well as the maximum and minimum overall.

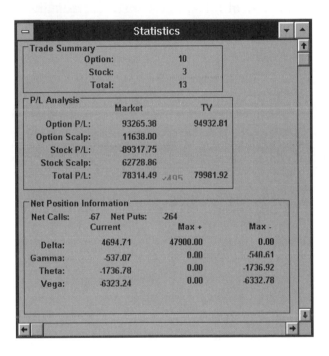

At the top of the statistics screen is a record of the total number of trades the student has performed in that trading day. There is a breakdown of total options trades and total underlier trades, as well as the total of both. The statistics page also breaks down the position into options only. For example, if the student is long 1,000 shares of the underlying, short ten of the April 90 calls, and long ten of the April 90 puts, the total calls and total puts will be equal to zero. If the position consists of short ten of the 90 calls and long 1,000 of the underlying, the total calls will be zero and total puts will be short ten, because this is a synthetic short put position. This allows the student to see a synthetic breakdown of his or her total position in options. It does not, however, give a breakdown by strike. It is a *net* option position. This is again a tool for the student to use in his or her education of options trading. The statistics screen also gives a profit and loss statement versus the market and versus the theoretical value. The statistics screen gives a breakdown of the option p/l, option scalp, stock p/l, stock scalp, and total p/l versus the market. The p/l for the theoretical value side only shows a theoretical value p/l for the option and a total p/l for the theoretical value. The most important part of the statistics screen is the breakdown of the Greeks (e.g., delta, gamma, vega, theta). This part of the screen shows the student what the overall risk profile looks like, it gives the student the ability to see what the current delta, gamma, vega, and theta positions are, as well as their maximum and minimum positions.

The statistics screen is similar to the order book in that its size cannot be altered by using the mouse. However, it can be moved around the screen to accommodate the student's preference.

MISCELLANEOUS

At the End of the Trading Day

When the trading day is over, a pop-up screen appears and signals the end of the day. It also asks the student whether he or she wishes to view the log. If the student clicks "NO," the simulator automatically ends the session and students find themselves back at the program manager.

Viewing the Trading Log

To view the trading log during the simulation, the student may click "File" on the formula bar at the top of the screen and choose "View Log." To exit the log, simply double click the top left-hand corner.

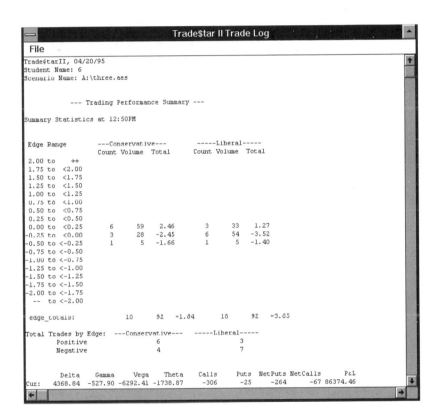

Exiting the Simulator

To exit the simulator, the student may click "File" from the formula bar and choose "Exit."

Saving an Unfinished Scenario

All unfinished scenarios are automatically saved when the student exits the simulator. When restarted, they continue from the point at which the student left off.

Restarting an Unfinished Scenario

To restart an unfinished scenario, the student must, after reentering the simulator, choose "Saved Scenarios" from the scenario screen. All saved scenarios are saved by the scenario name. Therefore, the student must remember which scenario he or she has been working on.

Final Notes

Students who encounter any difficulties must consult with a lab tech or the instructor before continuing.

GLOSSARY

advanced/decline line A measure of market movements composed of the cumulative total of differences between advancing issues (stocks whose prices are up on the day) and declining issues (stocks whose prices are down on the day) of securities prices.

American-style options Options that may be exercised any time prior to the expiration date.

ask The lowest currently stated acceptable price for a specific stock or commodity on the floor of an exchange. Also called the offer.

assignment The process by which the seller of an option is notified of the *buyer's* intention to exercise.

at-the-money An option in which the price of the underlying instrument is exactly the same as the strike price of the option.

bear Anyone who takes a pessimistic view of the forthcoming long-term trend in a market; that is, one who thinks that a market is or soon will be in a long-term downtrend.

bear market A long-term downtrend (a downtrend lasting months to years) in any market, especially in the stock market, characterized by lower intermediate lows interrupted by lower intermediate highs.

bear spread Any spread in which a fall in the price of the underlying security will theoretically increase the value of the spread.

bid An indication by an investor, trader, or dealer of the willingness to buy a security or a commodity at a certain price; also, the highest current such indication for a specific stock or commodity at any point in time.

bid and ask The current quote or quotation on the floor of any market exchange for a specific stock or commodity.

block A large amount of specific stock, generally 10,000 or more shares.

blue chip The common stock of an established industry leader whose products or services are widely known and that has a solid record of performance in both good and bad economic environments.

book value A measure of the net worth of a share of common stock.

bottom The lowest price within a market movement that occurs before the trend changes and starts moving up.

break A downward price movement that goes below previous important lows and continues to carry downward.

breakout An upward price movement that goes above previous important highs and continues to carry upward.

bull Anyone who takes an optimistic view of the forthcoming long-term trend in a market; that is, one who thinks that a market is or soon will be in a long-term uptrend.

bull market A long-term price movement in any market characterized by a series of higher intermediate highs interrupted by higher consecutive intermediate lows.

bull spread Any spread in which a rise in the price of the underlying security will theoretically increase the value of the spread.

butterfly spread An option position involving the simultaneous buying of an at-the-money option, selling two out-of-the money options, and buying one out-of-the-money option.

call option A short-term or medium-term contract that gives the purchaser the right but not the obligation to go long the underlying investment at the strike price on or before the option expiration date. An option seller receives the premium and assumes the obligation to go long or short the underlying investment at the strike price if the option is exercised.

commission The fee charged to a client by a registered broker for the execution of an order to buy or sell a stock, bond, commodity, option, etc.

correction An intermediate market price movement that moves contrary to the long-term trend.

covered position A combination of an underlying investment and an options transaction that is theoretically less risky than either individual part of the transaction.

delta The sensitivity (rate of change) of an option's theoretical value (assessed value) to changes in the price of the underlying instrument. Expressed as a percentage, it represents an equivalent amount of the underlying at a given moment in time. Calls have positive deltas. Puts have negative deltas.

Dow Jones Industrial Average (DJIA) The most widely used indicator of market activity, composed of an average of 30 large issues within the industrial sector of the economy.

Dow Jones Transportation Average (TRAN) The most widely reported indicator of stock activity in the transportation sector of the economy, composed of an average of 20 large issues.

Dow Jones Utility Average (UTIL) The most widely reported indicator of stock activity in the utility sector composed of 15 gas, electric, and power company issues.

earnings The net income available for common stock, divided by the number of shares outstanding, reported quarterly by most companies. Also earnings-per-share.

European-style options Options that may be exercised on the expiration date only.

exercise The process by which the buyer of an option notifies the seller of his or her intention to *take* delivery of the underlying instrument, in the case of a call, or *make* delivery, in the case of a put, at the specified exercise price.

exercise price The price at which the underlying instrument will be delivered in the event the option is exercised.

expiration The date an option contract becomes worthless. All buyers of options must indicate their desire to exercise by this date.

extrinsic value The price of an option less its intrinsic value. The entire premium of an option consists of extrinsic value.

fade Doing the opposite of the immediate market movement.

floor trader A member of an exchange who enters transactions for his or her own account from the floor of the exchange; synonymous with local.

glamour stock A favored, highly-traded stock, usually of an established company that has performed well and paid dividends in good times and bad.

growth stock A relatively speculative stock, usually one of a relatively new company that is expected to grow at a fast rate.

hedger One who transfers price risk by establishing equal and offsetting positions in different markets.

high The highest price a security or commodity reaches within a specified time period.

index futures Futures contracts traded on the basis of an underlying cash index or average.

in-the-money (ITM) A call is in-the-money if its strike is lower than the market price of the underlying instrument. A put is in-the-money if its strike price is higher than the market price of the underlying instrument.

intrinsic value (also called parity) The amount by which an option is in-the-money. Out-of-the-money (OTM) options have no intrinsic value.

long Position resulting from the purchase of a contract or instrument.

long-term trend Price movements tending to be generally up or generally down lasting over a period of months to years.

low The lowest price of a security or commodity reached during a specific time period.

margin The amount of equity (cash) as a percentage of market value of the underlying market interest held in a margin account.

neutral spread A position that has virtually no exposure to the conditions of a market. Also known as flat or square.

offer An indication by a trader or investor of the willingness to sell a security or commodity, or, in a quote, the current lowest price anyone is willing to sell a security or commodity.

out-of-the-money (OTM) An option that has no intrinsic value. A call is out-of-the-money if its strike price is higher than the current market price of the underlying. A put is out of the money if its strike price is lower than the current price of the underlying instrument.

over-the-counter (OTC) A market of stocks traded that are not listed on the major exchanges.

quote The current bid and offer for a security on the floor of the exchange on which it is traded.

put option An option contract that gives the buyer the right but not the obligation to sell the underlying investment at a specific price on or before a specific date.

ratio writing A market position using more than one option to hedge an investment position.

resistance Any price level that is deemed as a significant high in trading by the market and offers a place to sell the market.

Rho The sensitivity of an option's theoretical value to a change in interest rates.

S&P futures A futures index traded based on the S&P 500 Cash Index.

short A position resulting from the sale of a contract or instrument. To sell a contract without, or prior to, buying it.

spread A position that is both long and short in the same investment with different expiration dates or long or short different but similar investments.

stop order An order given to a broker that becomes a market order when the market price of the underlying instrument reaches or exceeds the specific price stated in the stop order.

straddle An options position consisting of a call and put in the same investment with the same expiration date and same strike price.

strangle A position in which one buys (or sells) both an out-of-money put and an out-of-money call.

support Any price level deemed as a significant low in trading by the market, which offers a place to buy the market.

synthetics Two or more trading vehicles combined to emulate another, or spread. Because the package involves different components, price is also different, but the risk is the same (there are exceptions, however).

technical analysis A method of market forecasting that relies exclusively on the study of past price and volume behavior to predict future price movements.

underlying The instrument (stock, future, or cash index) to be delivered when an option is exercised. The amount of underlying for each option contract depends on the security traded. For example, in stock options each contract represents 100 shares of the underlying stock.

volatility The degree to which the price of an underlying instrument tends to change over time. This variable, which the market implies to the underlying, may result from pricing an option through a model.

volume The number of shares of stocks that change ownership in a given time period.

FOR FURTHER READING

Abell, Howard. *The Day Trader's Advantage: How to Move from One Winning Position to the Next.* Chicago: Dearborn, 1997.

————. *Digital Day Trading: Moving from One Winning Stock Position to the Next.* Chicago: Dearborn, 1999.

————. *Risk Reward.* Chicago: Dearborn, 1998.

————. *Spread Trading.* Chicago: Dearborn, 1998.

Abell, Howard and Robert Koppel. *The Market Savvy Investor.* Chicago: Dearborn, 1999.

Barach, Roland. *Mindtraps: Mastering the Inner World of Investing.* Homewood, Ill.: Dow Jones-Irwin, 1988.

Baruch, Bernard M. *Baruch: My Own Story.* New York: Holt, Rinehart and Winston, 1957.

Bittman, James B. *Options for the Stock Investor: How Any Investor Can Use Options to Enhance and Protect Their Return.* New York: McGraw-Hill, 1995.

Chicago Board Options Exchange. *Option: Essentials, Concepts and Trading Strategies.* New York: McGraw-Hill, 1994.

Cottle, Charles M. *Options: Perception and Deception: Position Dissection, Risk Analysis and Defensive Trading Strategies.* New York: McGraw-Hill, 1996.

Douglas, Mark. *The Disciplined Trader.* New York: New York Institute of Finance, 1990.

Eng, William F. *The Day Trader's Manual: Theory, Art, and Science of Profitable Short-Term Investing.* New York: John Wiley, 1993.

Eng, William F. *Trading Rules: Strategies for Success.* Chicago: Dearborn, 1990.

Friedfertig, Marc and George West. *The Electronic Day Trader.* New York: McGraw-Hill, 1998.

Gann, W.D. *How to Make Profits Trading in Commodities.* Pomeroy: Lambert-Gann, 1976.

Houtkin, Harvey and David Waldman. *Secret of the SOES Bandit.* New York: McGraw-Hill, 1998.

Koppel, Robert. *Bulls, Bears, and Millionaires: War Stories of the Trading Life.* Chicago: Dearborn, 1997.

———. *The Intuitive Trader: Developing Your Inner Market Wisdom.* New York: John Wiley, 1996.

———. *The Tao of Trading.* Chicago: Dearborn, 1997.

Koppel, Robert and Howard Abell. *The Innergame of Trading: Modeling the Psychology of the Top Traders.* New York: McGraw-Hill, 1993.

———. *The Outer Game of Trading: Modeling the Trading Strategies of Today's Market Wizards.* New York: McGraw-Hill, 1994.

Le Bon, Gustave. *The Crowd: A Study of the Popular Mind.* 2nd ed. Atlanta, Ga.: Cherokee, 1982.

McMillan, Lawrence G. *Options as a Strategic Investment.* New Jersey: Prentice Hall, 1992.

Natenberg, Sheldon. *Option Volatility and Pricing Strategies.* New York: McGraw-Hill, 1988.

Schwager, Jack D. *Market Wizards: Interviews with Top Traders.* New York: New York Institute of Finance, 1989.

———. *The New Market Wizards: Conversations with America's Top Traders.* New York: Harper Business, 1992.

Thomsett, Michael C. *Getting Started in Options,* 3rd ed. New York: John Wiley and Sons, 1997.

INDEX

ABOUT THE AUTHOR

Howard Abell is chief operating officer of the Innergame Division of Rand Financial Services, Inc., concentrating on brokerage and execution services for institutional and professional traders. Abell is the co-author, with Bob Koppel, of *The Innergame of Trading* (McGraw-Hill, 1993) and *The Outer Game of Trading* (McGraw-Hill, 1994). He is the author of *The Day Trader's Advantage* (Dearborn, 1996), *Spread Trading* (Dearborn, 1997), *Risk Reward* (Dearborn, 1998) and *Digital Day Trading* (Dearborn, 1999).

For additional information about financial services or professional options training, please contact Howard Abell:

InnergameDivision/Rand Financial Services, Inc.
Chicago Board of Trade Building
141 West Jackson Blvd. Suite 1950
Chicago, IL 60604
800-726-3088
Fax: 312-559-8848
E-mail: hma@innergame.com
Visit our website at www.marketsavvyinvestor.com